TEN
ONE-ACT PLAYS

Ten
One-Act Plays

Selected and Edited by

Fred Eastman

Professor of Biography, Literature and Drama
Chicago Theological Seminary

Willett, Clark & Company
Chicago   New York
1937

FOREWORD

This collection seeks to provide between the covers of one volume ten one-act dramas of artistic quality and religious significance.

The combination is rare. One's chance of hitting on it, when he chooses only by the titles in a catalogue, is small. There are too many blanks to every prize. Hundreds of so-called religious dramas have somehow found their way into print. Most of them were written by persons who had something to say but had not studied the technique of dramatic structure. As a result their plays are weak and inept. They may be strong in " message " but they fail to convince. Theme triumphs; characterization falters.

It would seem, therefore, that an editor who had read a large proportion of the religious dramas now available might render some service if he selected a few which meet the tests of drama and of religion and bound them together in one book. The present compiler has attempted this task.

The tests of good drama which each of these ten plays had to pass were as follows:

Does it reach the emotions?

Do the characters seem real and worth knowing?

Is the central conflict adequate?

Does this conflict rise to a climax?

Does this conflict reflect a struggle common to the experience or observation of the audience?

Is the suspense maintained?

Do the characters have to make important choices?

Is the theme clear and worth while?

Is the solution convincing?

Does the play have a well built structure?

Is the dialogue concise?

Each play had to meet a further test, a religious one: *Does it have a religious effect upon an audience?* That is, does it send the audience away exalted in spirit, with a deepened sense of fellowship with God and man, and enriched in its understanding of the spiritual forces which struggle in men's souls? Obviously this is a much more difficult test than simply asking, "Does it deal with Bible characters, or with Christian teachings, or with missions?" What good is it to dress characters in Hebrew costumes or to put in their mouths archaic English or to have their conversation reek with pious sentiment if the audience goes away walking on no higher ground than when it entered? It is not the material of drama that makes it religious, but the *effect*. Not its roots, but its fruits.

The dramas which have passed these tests and are included in this volume come from the pens of skilled and experienced playwrights — which is what one would naturally expect. Mr. Lavery, Miss McFadden, Mrs. Hamlin and Mr. Wilde have all written longer plays which have been produced on Broadway as well as numerous short ones designed for church and school use. These four have also done considerable work in Hollywood studios. François Coppée was a distinguished French poet and dramatist. Mr. Mount's " Twentieth Century Lullaby " was a prize winner in an English playwriting contest in 1935. Dorothy Clarke Wilson has probably written more religious dramas than any other American writer. Louis Wilson (no relation to Dorothy Clarke Wilson) has at least a dozen plays and one manual to his credit. Elliot Field has dramatized many of the stories of modern religious work at home and abroad. From such disciplined dramatists come these plays.

For themes the playwrights have chosen the most important and vital issues of human life. " Monsignor's Hour," " Twentieth Century Lullaby," " The Great Choice," " Pawns " and " Peace I Give Unto You " all deal with some phase of war and peace. " The Lord's Prayer " faces the struggle to forgive; " Prize Money," the choice between escape and sacrificial service; " The

Tail of the Dragon," the conflict between nationalism and the kingdom of God. "Tidings of Joy" presents the Christmas story in modern guise. "He Came Seeing" pictures the cost of loyalty to a great cause.

The reader will find in the appendix an interpretation of the results of a recent survey on the extent and use of religious drama in the United States.

Grateful acknowledgment is here made to the following publishers for their permission to reprint the plays in this collection: to the Walter H. Baker Company for "Pawns," "Prize Money," "Peace I Give Unto You," "The Lord's Prayer" and "Twentieth Century Lullaby"; to Samuel French, Inc., for "He Came Seeing," "Tidings of Joy" and "The Great Choice"; to Dodd, Mead and Company, Inc., for "Monsignor's Hour"; and to the Missionary Education Movement for "The Tail of the Dragon." Without their cooperation, and that of the authors, this collection would not have been possible.

— F. E.

CONTENTS

A NOTE ON MODERN RELIGIOUS DRAMA

If you are to have live drama, said Laurence Housman, it must touch modern problems and conditions, even somewhat controversially perhaps. If the churches are to be alive they must show fight. If they dare not have drama that shows fight they are not going to have live drama, and the subject is closed. The question is: How can you set up live drama which will also be religious drama?

The real problem you are up against is a moral, a spiritual, problem. Is Christ still the Great Adventurer or is he only a reminiscence? Is to be Christian still the greatest social problem of today, or is it only a tradition? Are you going to put into your religious drama only those versions of Christianity which fit into our social system, which Caesar accepts and can make use of; or are you prepared to give Caesar the lie and to give institutional Christianity the lie when they bear false witness against what Christianity should stand for? On your answer to these questions depends whether or not you can have live drama in your churches.

If you mean to have live drama you must have the courage of your convictions and be ready to do the unfamiliar and unexpected thing. Put to yourselves this as a test: You are willing to have in your churches a mystery play, or something similar, from past ages; but are you equally willing to have a modern play, not merely a goody-goody play of pious, blameless characters, but a play of social conflict, like " Strife," or a play exposing legal cruelty, like " Justice," by Galsworthy? I do not mean necessarily those plays in particular, but plays generally as socially alive to our own times. Are you willing, incidentally, to have laughter? I think you must have it if your religious drama is to be free and worth while. In fact, not to be shocked at good laughter is one of the reforms in church convention most needed today.

If you ask me how to come by religious drama, take anything in the present social system you believe to be wrong and unchristian, tackle it ruthlessly and uncompromisingly, as you think it ought to be tackled. Show it up, make it as modern as you like, as controversial as you like; and if you have the dramatic gift and if your solution is a Christian solution, you have religious drama. You ask me for subjects? War, capital punishment, the soul-destroying system of our prisons, sweated labor, prostitution, the hardness of heart of the self-righteous, the color problem — out of all these you can get religious drama.

(From an address by Laurence Housman, as reported in the London *Times*.)

MONSIGNOR'S HOUR*

by

Emmet Lavery

CHARACTERS

ARTIST

LAWYER

MONSIGNOR MICHAEL CAREY

GABRIEL AUGUSTINE PAGNANI

CARDINAL PEREZ

MONSIGNOR AMATO

CARDINAL

FOUR SWISS GUARDS

Scene: A chamber in the art gallery of the Vatican in Rome.

Time: A day in early summer — perhaps ten or fifteen years from now.

MONSIGNOR'S HOUR

*Access to the chamber is gained by doors or arches at extreme
right and left of stage. There are several small paintings on
the walls of the room, which is distinguished by a great canvas
which takes up most of the wall upstage center. From where you
sit you can hardly see the little scroll that labels the painting
" The Key of Heaven," or underneath the words spoken at the
Last Supper: " My peace I leave with you, my peace I give unto
you. Let not your heart be troubled nor let it be afraid." A
particular radiance illuminates the figure of our Lord in this
group.*

(*At curtain the* LAWYER *and the* ARTIST *are entering.*)

LAWYER (*to smart young* ARTIST). All right, Sue. Maybe
the place is imposing. But what's behind it all? A thing has to
have more than size to be really big.

ARTIST (*gaily*). Oh, give it half a chance, Tommy. It does
something to you. It gives me a feeling of space, makes me feel
I want to stretch out and cover all Rome with a mural. Come
on, say you like it, Tommy. After all, you'll have to live with
it, too.

LAWYER. There's only one thing in this whole collection that
gets a rise out of me. That one there (*pointing to biggest canvas*). Whose is that?

ARTIST. Now you *are* coming on, Tommy. I never come
here without looking at it. And I don't think anyone knows a
thing about it. (*Quietly*) But you don't need to, do you? It's
the enigma of the collection — forgotten for centuries, we are
told; rescued from obscurity a few years ago by His Holiness.

(*The* LAWYER *and the* ARTIST *go closer to the painting and*

3

do not notice the arrival of MONSIGNOR MICHAEL CAREY, *a shrewd little Irish-American prelate, with a bit of purple V showing at the collar. He is accompanied by a young Italian of thirty-five, resplendent in an amazing collection of haberdashery — a policeman, no less, in mufti.*)

MONSIGNOR (*standing at threshold and drinking in the beauty of the room*). Ah, Gabriel, one hour in Rome is not enough!

PAGNANI (*in a pleasant, proprietary way*). We shall see, Monsignor, we shall see. Better one hour in Rome than an eternity somewhere else.

MONSIGNOR (*to* PAGNANI). My friend, what did you tell?

PAGNANI (*blandly*). What should I tell them but the truth: that you are a distinguished Father of the church!

MONSIGNOR. No, no, Gabriel. You must not say that. What would people think?

PAGNANI. And I said your name was Monsignor Carey, and that you were on an important mission — (MONSIGNOR *throws up his hands in despair and turns to some of the paintings.*)

LAWYER (*dryly*). His Holiness does see the folks sometimes, doesn't he? But it depends very much on who you are.

ARTIST. Oh, Tommy, please. Of course he sees people privately as well as publicly, lots of them.

LAWYER. Our best chance would be to see him in a crowd. When he does see people, he usually sees them all at once.

ARTIST. You're being rather horrid, Tommy.

LAWYER. Do you think you could see him alone or that I could?

ARTIST. What have we to see him about?

LAWYER. Suppose we did have something. Could we see him? Or does he only see important people?

ARTIST (*slowly, honestly*). I — I've never thought much about it. I just took it for granted that anyone who needed to could. . . .

LAWYER. I'll bet you can't get near him. Did you ever see

him? Did I? Could even the average priest walk in on him as if it really were "his father's house"?

ARTIST. I don't see why not.

LAWYER. Prove it.

ARTIST. It's not one of the things that's done most of the time. So how can I prove it?

LAWYER. I'll tell you. Let's ask the first priest we meet. Let's ask the one that was just here. (*Looks around gallery and sees* MONSIGNOR *upstage with back to audience in rapt contemplation of the big painting.*) Oh, I say, Father.

ARTIST. Please, Tommy, be reasonable.

MONSIGNOR. Yes, my friend?

LAWYER. I beg your pardon, but maybe you can help us. We can't seem to agree on something. I say you have to be somebody before you can see His Holiness. She says anyone can. Who's right?

MONSIGNOR. I am very sorry. I am not quite the person to settle that for you. I am not attached here. I am a stranger in Rome.

LAWYER. Suppose you wanted to see His Holiness in private, could it be arranged?

ARTIST. Tommy, this has gone far enough. Monsignor, I apologize. I am very sorry.

LAWYER (*stiffly*). Oh, if you feel that way about it, very well. I'll go along. I was only trying to get at the truth. (*Exits.*)

ARTIST (*to* MONSIGNOR). What am I going to do? I did want him to love Rome so.

MONSIGNOR (*smiling*). Give the young man another chance. He's certain to get over this little argument.

ARTIST. You don't know him. The last time we got in an argument — it was about the Supreme Court — we nearly broke off our engagement. . . . Is there any chance. . . ? How do people see His Holiness alone?

MONSIGNOR (*frankly*). You know, I've often wondered about

that too. But I haven't the slightest idea. (LAWYER *appears at entrance.*)

LAWYER (*very casually, having decided to be magnanimous*). Coming, Sue?

ARTIST (*wearily*). Oh, all right, Tommy. Good-by, Monsignor. And don't bother about — anything.

LAWYER (*with a manner almost patronizing*). It was silly of us to quarrel. Let's forget it. I guess I took unfair advantage of you. Why, I've found out that it's just about impossible. I guess Monsignor must have told you the same thing.

MONSIGNOR (*blithely*). I told her nothing of the sort.

ARTIST. Monsignor!

LAWYER. Oh, it's all right. I'm perfectly willing to overlook it.

MONSIGNOR. But I don't think we should permit His Holiness to be overlooked like this.

ARTIST. Do you really think that an audience can be arranged?

MONSIGNOR. My friends, I am a stranger in Rome. But I shall put you a sporting proposition. I shall put your challenge before the first prelate I meet — an audience for any one of the three of us — and we shall see what happens.

LAWYER (*uncomfortably*). Now you are making fun of me.

MONSIGNOR. If I lose, you can make fun of *me*.

ARTIST. Monsignor, we can't lose. I know we won't. Come along, Tommy. Here's where the north of Ireland takes a licking. (*They go out.*)

MONSIGNOR (*baffled*). Now what do you suppose made me do that?

PAGNANI. You are a padre after my own heart. And what a sense of humor! But you should not have joked so with the young Americans.

MONSIGNOR (*simply*). I wasn't joking. That's the trouble.

PAGNANI. Then you should have said nothing.

MONSIGNOR. That's exactly what I intended doing until the

young man became so patronizing. Surely I couldn't let *him* be in the position of *overlooking* the Holy Father?

PAGNANI (*impressively*). Il Papa has other things on his mind. Big things are in the wind. No general audiences for a week. Ambassadors come and go like so many pigeons. I myself have seen them. Something is in the air.

MONSIGNOR. Would one more pigeon bother him so much?

PAGNANI (*affectionately*). You are a strange one, my friend. I cannot understand you, but neither will I desert you. After all, I owe you something for the ticket to the gallery.

MONSIGNOR. Come, let us stand here a moment before this beautiful painting. It was for this that I stopped off in Rome.

PAGNANI. You have only one hour in Rome and you spend it on one painting.

MONSIGNOR. I heard about it from an old missionary. He told me to look at it, shut my eyes, and that then I would know what contentment really is.

PAGNANI. It is not accounted one of the great masterpieces.

MONSIGNOR. Hush, Gabriel. Can't you hear what is being said: (*very softly*) "My peace I leave with you, my peace I give unto you; not as the world giveth do I give unto you. Let not your heart be troubled nor let it be afraid"?

PAGNANI. I am listening, Monsignor.

MONSIGNOR. Now let us shut our eyes and pray. I was not meant to speak the way I did to that young man unless something were to come of it.

PAGNANI (*gallantly*). Very well, I have my eyes shut. Now let something come!

(*As* MONSIGNOR *and* PAGNANI *stand with heads bowed before the painting, a rather grim ecclesiastic swings through the gallery: His Eminence,* CARDINAL PEREZ, *in a heavy cloak, wearing the small red cap of a cardinal.* PEREZ, *an aristocrat to the fingertips, halts and surveys the two figures laconically.*)

PEREZ. So! This is what this picture does to people. Shuts their eyes to the realities of life.

MONSIGNOR (*opening eyes slowly*). I beg your pardon?

PAGNANI (*opening his eyes too — then with a gasp of recognition*). Your Eminence! Your blessing.

PEREZ (*blesses him. Then, grimly*). So someone remembers Perez, eh? Well, no matter. (*Goes closer to painting as MONSIGNOR and PAGNANI move away.*)

MONSIGNOR (*to PAGNANI*). There, I told you something would happen. Do — do you know His Eminence?

PAGNANI. Shh. He is the greatest diplomat since Merry del Val. I have helped his car through traffic many times.

MONSIGNOR. Excellent. You must introduce me at once.

PAGNANI. It cannot be done. I — I am no one. He is a prince of the church. And you — look here, Monsignor, who are you anyway?

MONSIGNOR (*sighing*). Does that really matter?

PEREZ (*swings around, grimly humorous*). Ah, Monsignor, I could not help hearing. When I came in, you were looking at this painting. Do you see anything in it?

MONSIGNOR. Yes indeed, Your Eminence, there is much to be seen.

PEREZ. Strange. Very strange. If that be the key to heaven I fail to grasp it.

MONSIGNOR. But it can mean only one thing. Do you not hear the words ringing in your ears, Your Eminence?

PEREZ. No, I can't, Monsignor. Not today, anyway. Perhaps it is well that I am going home.

MONSIGNOR (*trying to start a conversation*). And I've just come. Why, Your Eminence, you know you're the first person I've had a chance to talk to — that is, without an introduction. Now I suppose I won't see you again and I did so want to know . . . .

PEREZ. What is it you want to know, if you don't already know it?

MONSIGNOR (*quickly*). What is His Holiness like, personally I mean? Would it be possible . . . does he . . . does he ever smile, for instance?

PEREZ (*annoyed*). Monsignor, you go too far. (*Then softly*) Forgive me, I forgot you could mean nothing unpleasant since you hardly know me. Hmmm. I can say this to you, Monsignor: I should imagine that His Holiness does smile upon occasion and particularly this one. Only a moment ago he bade me look at this painting on my way out, the while he assured me, with a smile, that I would probably see nothing in it. Well, I still don't. So he is probably still smiling. Monsignor, good day. (*Sweeps out regally.*)

MONSIGNOR (*to* PAGNANI). And what does he mean by all that?

PAGNANI (*excitedly*). But it is all clear, these comings and goings of big men. (*Impressively*) Il Papa is talking peace!

MONSIGNOR. Are you sure? How would you know?

PAGNANI. Do you not read the papers? A month ago they said Cardinal Perez would go home in a huff. (*Drops voice to whisper*) Some say he may even give up the red hat. He and Il Papa have never seen eye to eye on peace.

MONSIGNOR (*sadly*). Small wonder he could see nothing in the painting. But you heard what he said: the pope smiles. Now if I could . . . .

PAGNANI. I shall never, never understand you. You can speak of whims when Il Papa carries such a crisis on his shoulders! You — you are as impossible as Cardinal Perez.

MONSIGNOR (*blithely*). Oh, no, my friend. You see, I understand the painting!

(MONSIGNOR AMATO, *a brisk and efficient Italian diplomat, enters the gallery. He wears a black cassock with purple buttons and a purple cloak — the dress worn by a domestic prelate on other than ceremonial occasions.*)

AMATO (*considerably agitated*). Monsignor! Signor! Permit me: a question, please. Cardinal Perez — has he passed this way? Or perhaps you do not know him?

MONSIGNOR (*blithely*). Oh yes, we know him. You can tell His Holiness that he found nothing of interest in the painting.

PAGNANI. Monsignor! One must be discreet.

AMATO (*icily*). I do not understand . . . that you should understand so completely. What is it you know about the painting? What is your business with Cardinal Perez? Monsignor, I do not believe we have the honor. . . .

MONSIGNOR. It's all very simple. I happened to be standing here when he came in. I never saw him before.

AMATO. But Cardinal Perez is not in the habit of speaking before strangers.

PAGNANI (*genially*). Ah, Monsignor Amato, there you have it. The little father, he has a way with him. That is all.

AMATO (*coldly*). And this person who knows my name — who is he?

MONSIGNOR. Gabriel? Why, Gabriel is a *policeman!* I met him this morning.

AMATO. A *policeman?*

MONSIGNOR. Of course. I had two tickets for the gallery. I did not want to come alone and so . . . .

AMATO. This is most irregular. I come here looking for Cardinal Perez and I find a policeman and a — a —

MONSIGNOR (*humbly*). A rural dean, Monsignor.

PAGNANI (*trying to impress* AMATO). That's what *he* says, but I don't believe him.

AMATO. And I find you parties to a most important . . . . Monsignor, your business here?

MONSIGNOR. I came to see the pictures — and — His Holiness!

PAGNANI (*to* AMATO). Yes, he's really here to see His Holiness. It is very droll.

AMATO. Impossible. Do you expect to find him in the galleries? Have you arranged for an audience?

MONSIGNOR. Oh no. I did not ask for an appointment.

PAGNANI. He thinks maybe he can see His Holiness just for the asking. (*Very confidentially*) A pilgrim put him up to it.

AMATO. What do you think would happen if we were to let people see His Holiness at will?

MONSIGNOR (*sighing*). I was afraid you'd think of that.

But what about him? Doesn't he want to let down the barriers once in a while, just to find out for himself whether the sun is still shining in people's hearts — without having to take it on the word of some diplomat?

AMATO. Ridiculous. Do you think His Holiness has time for such nonsense? Or that I have, either? How do I know that you are not an impostor?

MONSIGNOR. Monsignor jests with me.

AMATO. I shall take no chances. (*Goes to corridor and calls two guards, resplendent in uniform. They take position at doors.*) I must ask you both to remain here, under guard. You know entirely too much about the conversations of His Holiness and Cardinal Perez to be permitted complete liberty for the present.

PAGNANI (*to* MONSIGNOR). Now, you see. He wants to arrest *me* — me, a policeman. What will my chief say? (*Then to* AMATO *in wily fashion*) Most reverend Monsignor, the situation looks bad. That I will admit. My friend has no credentials at the moment. Indeed he is not accredited at all. He is only passing through. (*Softly*) And I don't really know who he is. But no sane man could be that simple without being somebody.

MONSIGNOR. Thank you, my friend.

PAGNANI (*blandly*). Are they not delightful, these Americans? So droll. Make no mistake about it, reverend Monsignor. Gabriel Augustine Pagnani knows a churchman when he sees one.

AMATO (*considerably vexed*). I am perplexed. I cannot comprehend. Nothing like this has ever happened before. You must remain here for a few moments for further questioning. You understand: I do not like to make a mistake. This is not a time for mistakes. I shall return presently. (*Exits quickly.*)

MONSIGNOR (*eyeing guard at one exit, then guard at the other*). Have I seen him somewhere before — in the rotogravures perhaps?

PAGNANI. Ah, Monsignor Amato is here, there, everywhere. He is, my friend, one of the secretaries in the papal household.

And if you aren't what I think you are, this little prank may go hard with us.

MONSIGNOR. But, Gabriel, why will you insist on making me something that I am not?

PAGNANI (*very persuasively*). You *could* be somebody, just as well as not. Ah yes, the more I think of it, the more I'm sure you are — at least, until we get out of here.

MONSIGNOR (*smiling*). You Italians are incorrigible. You all talk like Dante and act like Lorenzo the Magnificent.

PAGNANI. Much better. We shall make somebody of you yet. You have, my friend, the soul for adventure.

MONSIGNOR. Adventure, like beauty, is in the eye of the beholder. And for the present, I can find all I need in this one canvas.

PAGNANI (*looking at painting*). Peace! A poor man's dream, eh? A bird on the wing, that. So easy to catch with the brush on a painting, but in life? Santa Maria, it is out of our hands. Psst. Look, Monsignor, the guards are gone. (*Goes to arch*) Perhaps we had better go before they come back.

MONSIGNOR. I am in no hurry. You may go if you wish.

PAGNANI (*nervously*). Perhaps it would be wise if I find someone to intercede for us . . . (*edging toward arch*).

MONSIGNOR. By all means.

PAGNANI (*in anguish*). Ah, but you think that I desert you, I — Gabriel Augustine Pag —

MONSIGNOR (*quietly*). No, my friend, I am afraid I am not even thinking of you at all. And I would like to be alone.

PAGNANI. If Monsignor insists. . . .

MONSIGNOR. Consider that I have insisted.

PAGNANI (*with relieved alacrity*). I bow to Monsignor's wish but I return, never fear. I go — yes, I go, but only that I may return. (*With smart click of heels*) Good Father — arrivederci! (*Exits.*)

(MONSIGNOR *is left alone and stands upstage, lost in admiration for the painting. After a few seconds, a tall figure appears*

*at arch L. He wears an all-enveloping dark cloak and a small
white skullcap. A man of simple majesty, with jet black hair
and noble features, there is a serenity about him that is com-
pelling. Surprised to discover that he is not alone in the gallery,
he moves up quietly alongside* MONSIGNOR *and examines the
painting.)*

CARDINAL (*softly*). Ah — "the tranquillity of things in
order!"

MONSIGNOR (*turning quickly*). Oh, I beg your pardon. I
thought I was alone, Your — Your Eminence?

CARDINAL (*smoothly*). I had forgotten that my white cap
would identify me so readily.

MONSIGNOR. That would make you a cardinal of the Domini-
cans surely. Oh, I am deeply honored, Your Eminence.

CARDINAL (*gently*). Does it matter so much who I am, Monsignor, or who you are?

MONSIGNOR (*delighted*). But of course not. Those were my
very words just now to Monsignor Amato. (*Cautiously*) Do
you know Monsignor Amato?

CARDINAL (*smiling*). We are acquainted.

MONSIGNOR. For some reason he suspects me — of I know
not what. Perhaps he will arrest you, too, if he finds you here
with me.

CARDINAL. I imagine we shall not be troubled by Monsignor
Amato.

MONSIGNOR. I wouldn't want to get you into trouble. The
guards he left with me may come back.

CARDINAL (*smiling*). I hardly think we shall be troubled by
the guards either. . . . I should not mention it to you, but one
must have someone with whom to share a secret: the pope is not
in his apartments. They are looking all over for him!

MONSIGNOR. Your Eminence! Is anything wrong?

CARDINAL. Just between ourselves, Monsignor, I think he
wanted to get away from Monsignor Amato!

MONSIGNOR. I knew it. He's a man after my own heart.

CARDINAL (*softly*). Sometimes I wonder if anyone knows what is really in the heart of His Holiness. He has so few intimates.

MONSIGNOR. Ah, that must be hard. At least it would for me, for I love people.

CARDINAL. Ah, Monsignor, what made you seek out this picture?

MONSIGNOR. The priest whose chapel I shared at Stresa told me not to miss " The Key of Heaven."

CARDINAL (*pleased*). So there are a few who do not forget? (*Goes up closer to painting*) Every so often I come back to look at it. Sometimes I think I have its full meaning clear before me, only to find that it eludes me.

MONSIGNOR (*quietly*). " My peace I leave with you." It seems simple enough. The words are plain.

CARDINAL. But how far — how far must one go?

MONSIGNOR. If there is no limit to God's charity, if he is infinity itself, who are we to put limitations on the peace which was his legacy to us?

CARDINAL. True, Monsignor, but times have changed since first those words were said.

MONSIGNOR. Times have changed. Only God remains — the same.

CARDINAL (*sitting wearily in tall chair beneath painting*). The only trouble with your philosophy, Monsignor, is that it is so true. The theory is unimpeachable. But we are not dealing with theories. (*Impressively*) Even now — perhaps you have heard — the whole question is before us. The new conference at Geneva is to adjourn tomorrow. Nothing has been accomplished. The race for arms begins anew. What are we to do that men may live in peace?

MONSIGNOR. Why, we must end war forever.

CARDINAL. And yet there is no war, at least not yet.

MONSIGNOR. The time for the Prince of Peace to speak is while there still is peace.

CARDINAL. I know, Monsignor. All the arguments are good. They have been good for centuries . . . but I am not convinced that too positive action might not lose us as much as it would gain.

MONSIGNOR (*disdainfully*). Oh, expediency: thy name is war.

CARDINAL (*aroused*). Monsignor!

MONSIGNOR (*abashed*). Your pardon, Your Eminence. I forgot myself for a moment.

CARDINAL (*quietly*). You are to be congratulated — and envied. Monsignor, you arrive in Rome at a critical moment. This afternoon His Holiness is to meet the Congregation of Extraordinary Ecclesiastical Affairs and draft a program of policy. Already he has under consideration two possible forms for an encyclical to the entire world. One is a prayer for peace — the other would enjoin the faithful from ever bearing arms in war again!

MONSIGNOR. God be praised!

CARDINAL. His Holiness, you will be pleased to learn, has at times inclined to your views, being of the opinion that no war can be a just war today.

MONSIGNOR. Ah, this is a happy day for me, Your Eminence.

CARDINAL (*coldly*). But I have been against him on the proposition.

MONSIGNOR (*impulsively*). Oh, but you're wrong, Your Eminence. You mustn't do that. People all over the world are looking up to the Holy Father. He's the last hope of millions who never want to fight again. You must let him know that. You must tell him what we ordinary people are thinking. You must let me see him. (*Excitedly*) Yes, that's it, you must let me see him, for now I have a good reason for seeing him.

CARDINAL. You will excuse me, Monsignor, I do not understand.

MONSIGNOR. Oh, I had an argument with a young man who said His Holiness was so remote, an ordinary person could never see him. And I found myself telling him that he was all wrong.

There's a girl in it, too, who is going to marry the young man, and she thinks it's no harder to see His Holiness than it is for her to talk with her own parish priest. A little fanciful maybe, but I did want to confound that young man.

CARDINAL (*smiling*). Would you turn the Vatican upside down for just one soul?

MONSIGNOR. I'm not so sure I can get his soul that easily, but if I could, wouldn't it be worth the effort? The only thing that bothered me was that none of us had any special reason to seek an audience with His Holiness. (*Very simply*) But now I have. Don't — don't you think he could see me, just for a minute even?

CARDINAL (*tolerantly*). I am certain that they would never permit you to see him — today of all days.

MONSIGNOR. But it must be today. No other day will do. He's going to decide things today. You just said so yourself.

CARDINAL. And do you think he would really listen to you?

MONSIGNOR (*vigorously*). He must listen to someone. If he listens to you, why can't he listen to me? . . . If I were pope for only five minutes, I'd fix things. I know what it is people want. And I'd get it for them too.

CARDINAL. Very well, Monsignor. Let us put it to the test. (*Rising from chair*) I have a little game to play with people occasionally. However, I should warn you that few of them are equal to it. Now, are you ready?

MONSIGNOR (*puzzled*). Yes, Your Eminence.

CARDINAL (*gesturing for* MONSIGNOR *to take chair*). Excellent. Now, Monsignor, suppose that *you* are pope! What then?

MONSIGNOR (*genuinely shocked*). Oh, Your Eminence, you suppose too much.

CARDINAL. You see — what did I tell you?

MONSIGNOR. But I would not think of presuming. . . .

CARDINAL (*serenely*). Is any life that is an imitation of Christ presumptuous?

MONSIGNOR (*suddenly*).   All right.   I will then — if it please Your Eminence!

(MONSIGNOR *takes the chair and gradually, as he speaks, he assumes more and more of the traditional mannerisms of the pontiffs. At first, perhaps, they seem to fit him strangely, even humorously, but there shines through the gentle masquerade the spirit of a great soul, and the result is a magnificent dignity that makes you surrender to the mood as easily as it does the* CARDINAL. *As the scene advances the two characters change subtly for the moment and the* CARDINAL *follows while the* MONSIGNOR *leads. Literally — as well as spiritually — they have changed places with each other.*)

MONSIGNOR.   Perhaps it is time to remember that each one of us in this life is made to the image and likeness of God.   (*Solemnly*) And by the same token no man should be permitted to slay another, lest he slay not only his brother but his God as well.

CARDINAL (*humbly*).   Shall it be said then that a man must yield his life to any man who may wish to take it?

MONSIGNOR.   No.   One need not surrender to the first intruder who would take home or family from him.   But as between *nation* and *nation*, something must be done to protect the individual from exploitation by the state!

CARDINAL.   But there have been righteous wars, wars that won liberty for people when nothing else could give it to them.

MONSIGNOR.   The cycle changes.   The wars that gave us liberty are in the past.   The wars that take our liberty are before us.

CARDINAL.   Suppose you could teach men that there is more freedom today in peace than there is in war.   Suppose they believed it with all their hearts.   But if someone questioned their honor, what then?

MONSIGNOR.   The world will always invite men to *die* for their honor.   How long must it be before people wonder why they are not exhorted to *live* for their honor?

CARDINAL. The people are afraid. They are afraid they will be called cowards.

MONSIGNOR. Nobody who can face the truth is a coward. And the truth is that no one will win the next war. (*Speaking softly but firmly and with all the emphasis of a pontiff sensing the gravity of an approaching crisis*) There are no more civilians. All fight, all are slain: women, children, aged and sick. It is no longer army against army. It is people against people. Everyone fights — and everyone loses.

CARDINAL. If we are to ask three hundred million people of our faith not to bear arms, it may mean persecution for many.

MONSIGNOR (*serenely*). The church and persecution are no strangers. The only question before us is not what will happen if we do this; but, is it the right thing to do?

CARDINAL. It may mean the massacre of innocent thousands.

MONSIGNOR (*gravely*). Yes, the price is often the same for peace or for war. But wouldn't you rather pay it for peace?

CARDINAL. But suppose your command could not be enforced! Suppose the people do not obey!

MONSIGNOR (*wisely*). How little you know the people of this world. They are merely waiting for someone to give the order — the order not to fight.

CARDINAL. And why should we succeed where the League of Nations has failed?

MONSIGNOR. Because we speak to *people* and the league speaks to *governments*. We speak to the individual, first and last.

CARDINAL (*perturbed*). Kings may fall. Governments may be wiped out. Mobs will have their day. If we seek to change the world overnight, who stands at our shoulder to preserve order?

MONSIGNOR. God, of course. Is he not with us " all days, even unto the end of time "?

CARDINAL. You have no qualms. How can you be so sure that we are not meant to leave things as they are?

MONSIGNOR (*quietly*).   Our God is not the Lord-of-things-as-they-are but the Lord-of-things-as-they-should-be.

CARDINAL (*excitedly*).   But will they choose God above Caesar?

MONSIGNOR.   Why not?   What kind of a world has Caesar made for them?   (*Now courageously, as a pontiff might before a great council*) Your Eminence, this life that God gives us comes at too great a cost to be thrown away on the altars of mere nations.   It is God's and God's alone to take.   He made it.   It belongs to him forever and ever.   The time is come for us to say to each country of the world: You can take this life of ours, if you will, in the name of peace, but you can never have it for war. (*Pause*) Let others, if they choose, take the *profits* out of war — it is for us to take the *people* out of war.

(*The* LAWYER *and the* ARTIST *enter the gallery again.* MON-SIGNOR *slowly emerges from his daydream and gets up from chair; the* CARDINAL *moves to the opposite corner of gallery and stands with back to the others.*)

ARTIST.   Take St. Peter's altogether and do you know what you have?   It's a testament to beauty, a tribute of joy to a Creator from his creatures.   It's David dancing before the Ark!

LAWYER.   But what's it like underneath?   Suppose it were all only ornament.

ARTIST (*laughing*).   But it isn't.   Just listen to the people on the street.   What do they call His Holiness?   King?   No, it's " Father."

LAWYER (*sighting* MONSIGNOR *near the entry L.*).   Monsignor!   We almost forgot all about you.   Well, which of us was right?

ARTIST.   Oh, Tommy, what could you expect in so little time?

MONSIGNOR (*still somewhat dazed*).   I beg your pardon . . . oh, yes, I remember.   Dear me, it seems such a long time ago — and so very unimportant.

LAWYER. I knew it couldn't be arranged. I suppose it was hardly fair of me to urge the point.

MONSIGNOR (*his mind on other matters*). We must remember that we were — jesting, if you will, about a mere whim. But this is not a day for whims.

CARDINAL (*who has turned and listened to the conversation with much interest, now joins the group. There is no one else in the gallery.*) On the contrary, Monsignor, a most excellent day for whims. Is this the young couple of whom you spoke?

ARTIST. Monsignor! Then you did try?

MONSIGNOR. Yes, Your Eminence, these are the young people. But I crave your indulgence. I — I did not realize the demands on His Holiness, today of all days.

CARDINAL. But there are other days. Tell me, signor, would it mean so much to you to see His Holiness?

LAWYER (*diffidently*). You make me feel a little small when you put it that way, sir — I mean, Your Eminence. (*Then proceeds with likable stubbornness*) But it would mean a great deal. Just to see him would settle something for me forever.

CARDINAL (*lightly*). Then, by all means, let us consider it arranged.

ARTIST. Oh, Your Eminence, how kind of you.

MONSIGNOR. We impose on your good nature.

CARDINAL. It is a little irregular, perhaps — but why not? Perhaps it will be good for His Holiness as well as for the young man.

LAWYER. You mean it can really be done? That is *all* there is to it?

CARDINAL. But of course. Return here at the same hour tomorrow and I shall arrange to have you presented. I — I shall meet you here myself.

ARTIST. Monsignor — Your Eminence — how marvelous of you both!

CARDINAL. It is a little thing. One would do much more for Monsignor. Good day, my dear friends, and God bless you!

LAWYER. Good-by, Monsignor. I'll never forget this. (*Then to* ARTIST *on way out*) But, Sue, what *will* I talk to him about? I guess I haven't a single thing to say!

MONSIGNOR (*beaming*). I am so happy for them, Your Eminence. What a lesson this is going to be to that young man!

CARDINAL. Truly, Monsignor, it is a day for whims, a day with the zest of adventure in it. I shall look forward to that audience. You, of course, must be there too.

MONSIGNOR (*sighing*). If that were only possible. But my boat leaves Naples in the morning and I have overstayed my time already. The pity of it too. (*Then brightly*) It must be my penance for leaving just one hour for Rome. (*Guards appear at entry R. and take up positions in the gallery.*)

MONSIGNOR. There, you see, Your Eminence. They've come back for me.

CARDINAL. I hear Monsignor Amato in the corridor. Give me just a moment with him, Monsignor. It is I for whom he comes — I am late for a meeting again and he won't like it — but if you will wait at that end of the gallery. . . . (MONSIGNOR *withdraws to opposite end of gallery, just as more guards enter from both ends, and the* CARDINAL *meets* AMATO *at extreme R.*)

AMATO (*bowing respectfully*). If you are ready, Your —

CARDINAL (*checking him swiftly, prevents him from disclosing his true identity by name, although Amato's extreme deference might well have given the masquerade away to anyone less excited than* MONSIGNOR). Well, what is it this time, Monsignor Amato?

AMATO (*almost severely*). The Congregation — it has been waiting one hour.

CARDINAL. Let us hope the Congregation has possessed its soul in patience.

AMATO. On the contrary, it is most impatient. Their Eminences will at least expect some word. . . .

CARDINAL. Very well. The word shall be: Peace. Peace on earth and good will to men.

MONSIGNOR (*very softly*). God be praised.

AMATO (*in protest*). But it was agreed that now is not the time. . . .

CARDINAL. Then there must be a new agreement.

AMATO. The situation is grave. . . . There are new advices from Berlin . . . Vienna. . . .

CARDINAL (*significantly*). There are also new advices — from America!

AMATO (*stiffly — with a sharp look at* MONSIGNOR). Monsignor! My apologies. I was not aware of your mission.

CARDINAL. It shall be communicated to you and the Congregation in due time. Advise Their Eminences that I shall be with them shortly. (AMATO *bows stiffly and goes out, but the guards remain.*)

MONSIGNOR (*delightedly*). That means you stand with His Holiness. Oh then he will win the day! But, Your Eminence, I have no mission.

CARDINAL. You shall be an ambassador without portfolio. You shall come with me now to the meeting of the Congregation.

MONSIGNOR. I couldn't do that, Your Eminence. What have I to offer Their Eminences?

CARDINAL. You have the divine gift, a sense of proportion. I must have you with me. It will not be easy to make them understand, at first.

MONSIGNOR. Never fear, Your Eminence. We're on the side of the angels.

(*Offstage there is heard the gentle tolling of bells in a nearby chapel where an organist is playing at vespers.*)

CARDINAL. And they will listen to us, Monsignor, even as I have listened to you, for have you considered: Who is it that speaks inside us today? Is it you? Is it I? It seems to me that never before have I seen so clearly that there can be no brotherhood of man without the fatherhood of God. Come, Monsignor, let us go and pray for peace to men of good will. (CARDINAL *and* MONSIGNOR *start off L., when a slight commotion is heard R. and* PAGNANI *enters with a flurry of exclamations.*)

PAGNANI. Monsignor! Monsignor! You must not leave yet. I have just discovered great news. His Holiness is in this wing, even now!

MONSIGNOR (*turning abruptly from the* CARDINAL *who remains L., goes R. to* PAGNANI). Gabriel! Are you sure? What can it mean? Do you suppose I can see him before I go?

PAGNANI (*struggling with two guards who are not sure what they should do with him*). Can you not see I am a friend of the Monsignor? (*The guards withdraw a bit. Then to* MONSIGNOR) The whole gallery is full of guards. All the pilgrims have been escorted out. He may be on the way here at this moment. This painting, they say, is his favorite.

MONSIGNOR. Ah, Gabriel, this is my day of days. And I almost forgot: we have a great friend at court, a distinguished prince of the church. Come, Gabriel, I must present you to His Eminence. (*Then to* CARDINAL, *who has not quite turned full face to* PAGNANI) I declare, Your Eminence, I don't even know your name! (*More guards enter, quietly take up positions.*)

CARDINAL. Nor I yours, Monsignor. But does it matter? My name — it is —

PAGNANI (*as* CARDINAL *turns to him full face gives a joyous shout of recognition and falls to his knees*). Il Papa! Il Papa mio! Viva Il Papa!

MONSIGNOR (*incredulous*). Your Eminence? Your Eminence? (*Then in complete amazement, scanning the additional guards who now throng the gallery*) Your — Your Holiness? (*Drops to knees.*) Forgive me — forgive me.

POPE (*from his shoulders a prelate lifts the black cloak, disclosing his white cassock and his papal cross*). Ah, Monsignor, what is there to forgive? (*He lifts* MONSIGNOR *to his feet.*) Was what you said any the less true because you said it to the Bishop of Rome?

MONSIGNOR (*awed*). But, Your Holiness, I ordered you around as if you were my own curate!

POPE. And Monsignor Amato was for sequestering you as a dangerous diplomat. Surely the honors are even, Monsignor.

MONSIGNOR. But I'm not a diplomat at all, Your Holiness. That's what I've been trying to tell everyone all along. You see — I'm — just a parish priest, nothing more.

POPE. What more is there one could be? What, think you, am I, Monsignor? I am no more than pastor, with a world for my parish.

MONSIGNOR (*humbly*). You are the Vicar of Christ on earth. You are the Prince of Peace. Your blessing, Your Holiness. (MONSIGNOR *kneels. So, too, do* PAGNANI *and all present.*)

POPE. What was it you said, Monsignor? " The time for the Prince of Peace to speak is while there is still peace "? (*Blesses all present.*) I bless for peace, Monsignor, and I act for peace. God be with us.

(*The organ music dies down very softly as the* POPE *once more lifts* MONSIGNOR *to his feet.*)

MONSIGNOR. Ah, Your Holiness, God's always with us when we go God's way.

POPE. Come, Monsignor, shall we walk his way together?

(*The* POPE *and* MONSIGNOR *start out slowly together while guards come stiffly to attention and* PAGNANI *stands beaming with pride, just as if he had arranged it all. Music swells to a gentle crescendo.*)

CURTAIN

TIDINGS OF JOY*

by

Elizabeth McFadden

CHARACTERS

MARY DOE — *? Lila Cooper* (handwritten)

THE BABY — *? Hedrick* (handwritten)

JOSEPH DOE

A CITY MARSHAL — *Keith* (handwritten)

AL, *his helper* — *Herbert* (handwritten)

TIM, *a second helper* — *Robert* (handwritten)

DICK *Jerry* (handwritten)
SALLIE *Wilford* (handwritten)
TED
ALICE
HAL *Luther* (handwritten)
LUCY
JOHN *Leo* (handwritten)
BOBBIE
MAGGIE

} *Children from the neighborhood church, out singing Christmas carols. The boys may be Boy Scouts in uniform. The girls may be Girl Scouts or Camp Fire Girls, if desired.*

MR. CHASE, *from the neighborhood church* — *Ben* (handwritten)

MISS DUNCAN, *a Red Cross nurse*

A POLICEMAN — *Hubert* (handwritten)

Any number of other CHILDREN, *Christmas* WAITS, *as desired.*

Scene: A basement room in a poor tenement in any town where the play is given.

Time: Christmas Eve. This year.

NOTE ON MUSIC

The author desires to make acknowledgment to Humphrey Milford and to the Oxford University Press of London for permission to use the carols which are quoted in "Tidings of Joy." They are all taken from the collection of over two hundred carols, ancient and modern, entitled *The Oxford Book of Carols,* compiled and edited by Percy Dearmer, R. Vaughan Williams and Martin Shaw, and published, complete with music, by the Oxford University Press, London.

This book may be ordered, together with the copies of the play, from Samuel French, Inc., through any of its offices in New York, Los Angeles, London or Toronto. Price, $2.50.

TIDINGS OF JOY

A poor tenement room, spotlessly clean and somehow made into a home. The high window, in the wall right, which looks out on the street, is protected by cheap curtains, white and fresh. The rear wall has a door right center leading to the entrance hall and street; a door left center leading to the inner room; between the two a neat kitchen dresser. The left side wall has an open hearth, but without a fire when the play begins. Down center is a kitchen table covered with a dark-colored cloth. To the right of it is Joseph's chair, to the left of it is Mary's chair and to the left of Mary's chair is the baby's cradle. It is evident that Mary's chair has been made by an amateur carpenter. It is crudely constructed of unpainted wood, and yet there is something thronelike in its proportions and lines. Every effort has been made by the maker to have it comfortable. It is furnished with red cushions. There is a footstool before it. The cradle also is homemade but somehow has a delicate beauty of design. The quilt hanging over the sides is in a lovely color. The gray plaster walls have a couple of cheap pictures. On the mantel over the fireplace is an unlit candle stuck in a cheap holder. On the table stands a milk bottle holding a couple of faded flowers, perhaps a sprig of green.

It is a dull winter afternoon, the last hour before dusk.

MARY *sits in her chair, busy with some bit of sewing and watching the baby, which is in the cradle beside her. She is a slender young woman. Her face has great spirituality. As she sews on, there comes the sound of children's voices, singing off down the street.*

CHORUS (*sings*).
What tidings bringest thou, messenger,
Of Christes birth this jolly day?

A SINGLE CLEAR, SWEET BOYISH VOICE (*sings*).

A babe is born of high nature,
The Prince of Peace that ever shall be,
Of heaven and earth he hath the cure,
His lordship is eternity.

(MARY, *her attention caught, sits, needle suspended, rapt and happy, as the song draws nearer.*)

CHORUS.

What tidings bringest thou, messenger,
Of Christes birth this jolly day?

BOY.

Such wonder tidings ye may hear,
That man is now made Goddes peer,
Whom sin hath made but
Fiendes prey.

(*The childish voices have been drawing nearer, now they pass in the street outside. As they begin to grow fainter:*)

CHORUS.

What tidings bringest thou, messenger,
Of Christes birth this jolly day?

BOY.

A wonder thing is now befall
That King that formèd star and sun,
Heaven and earth and angels all,
Now in mankind is new begun!

(*The song rings on and on, fainter and fainter, till it fades to silence. MARY turns to the baby and smiles at him.*)

MARY.   Baby, it's Christmas Eve! And mother hasn't anything to give you! (*Her eyes fall on the sewing in her lap. She picks it up and holds it out to him.*) Oh, yes! This is for you! I'll give you this. (*She smiles brightly at the child. Steps approach along the street, pass the window and turn in at the outer door. MARY recognizes them.*) There's your daddy! Walking fast! Perhaps he has something for you! Perhaps — he's found a job!

(JOSEPH DOE *enters R.C. A manly-looking young fellow, his clothing clean but patched. His expression is anxious.*)

MARY. Joe!

JOE (*looking around as though expecting to find something he dreaded to see*). Mary! Has anyone — been — here?

MARY. No. Why? Who would be here?

JOE (*takes a restless turn or two across the floor, then turns to her with decision*). Mary, you've got to know. (*He takes a paper out of his pocket and hands it to her.*) That came three days ago. I thought I could fix it without your knowing about it, but — I can't. I can't.

MARY. But what is it, Joe?

JOE. Read it.

MARY (*bending over the paper, reading it aloud hesitatingly as though she did not understand it*). "Municipal Court of the city of ——, the 5th district. The Grand Street Real Estate Corporation, landlord, against Joseph Doe, tenant, —— street. The people of the state of ——: To the tenant, Joseph Doe, above named and described, in possession of the premises hereinafter described or claiming possession thereof: — Greeting." (*She looks up at* JOE *in bewilderment.*) "Greeting!" What's it all about, Joe?

JOE. You're coming to the gist of it now. Read the next sentence.

MARY (*reading*). "You are hereby required forthwith to remove from the premises designated and described as follows to wit: the two rooms in the basement of the house and premises known as —— street — " (*She looks up at him with terror in her face.*) "Forthwith to remove — " Joe! *Get out of here?* "*Forthwith*"? Joe!

JOE. It's what they call a writ of eviction. I hadn't the heart to tell you. Now *I've got to!*

MARY. When did it come?

JOE. Three days ago.

MARY. What are we going to do about it?

JOE. I've been doing everything I could think of — for the last three days. They tell you down there at the bottom of the paper to come to court. I went there day before yesterday. They said we'd have to get out. I been up to the office where we rented this place. They said they'd waited long enough. They gave me till this afternoon. . . . (*He sinks down in the chair R. of table with a sense of collapse half exhaustion, half despair, and drops his head in his hands.*)

MARY (*swiftly conscious of his lonely struggle to shield her, goes to him, puts her arms around him*). Joe! Dear! You should have told me. Not borne it all alone.

JOE. I don't care for myself. But what am I going to do about you and him?

MARY (*stands, looking all about her at the separate pieces of furniture as though seeing them in a new light, in which each presents a problem. Last of all she looks at the baby in the crib. Her expression grows dazed, panic-stricken.*) We can't " remove forthwith "! We haven't any place to go! (*JOE shakes his head without looking up. He cannot face her eyes.*) What would they do — if we don't go?

JOE. They'll — put us out.

MARY. Out where?

JOE. Out on the street.

MARY. Tonight? (*JOE nods his head. She turns and looks at the window that gives on the street, then back at the crib and the baby.*)

JOE. I've just come from the office of those real-estate people. They said the men were on their way here. So I hurried back.

MARY. I can't believe they would be so cruel.

JOE. Ha! You don't know 'em. This isn't Millbrook, Mary, where everybody knows everybody else and folks are neighborly. This is a big town, and the devil take the hindermost.

MARY (*looking at him with a lovely expression of maternal*

tenderness). Dear Joe! You are so tired. That makes it seem worse than it really is. I think if we talk to them when they come and tell them about the baby —

JOE. Yeah! I been a-telling them about the baby, and you just a kid yourself and just out of the hospital — much they care! (*She goes to him again and lays her hand on his shoulder in a comforting caress. He rises and puts his arms around her in a frantic desire to protect her.*) Mary! When we married I told you I'd always take care of you!

MARY (*in a voice that is liquid silver*). You will, Joe! I'm not afraid. I'm never lonely nor frightened any more — since I have you. (*She does her best to pull herself together and think constructively.*) We must find a place to stay tonight. To-morrow things won't look so bad.

JOE. I've been looking for a place. . . . (*Again he makes the gesture of failure.*) I don't know what to tell you to do!

MARY (*sitting on the arm of his chair, her arm around him, his head against her shoulder. Her voice is determinedly cheer-ful.*) We must be very practical and decide just what to do when they come.

JOE. I'd like to throw them out.

MARY. No. That wouldn't help. First, there's the unem-ployment relief — we read about that in the papers.

JOE. I went there yesterday, Mary.

MARY. What did they say?

JOE. It's just for folks who belong here. They said we never should have left home.

MARY. Did you tell them that you came because you were offered a good job?

JOE. They said that when it didn't pan out we should have gone right back to Millbrook, six months ago. They're out! I tell you the people here are hard-boiled.

MARY. Joe, I'm sure that if we went out there and stood on the street corner and asked the first person that passed to help us — he'd do it.

JOE (*sits silent for a moment and when he does speak his voice is hoarse with the agony of his experience*). I — stood out there, this noon, Mary, for more than an hour. I tried to speak to a dozen people.

MARY. Joe! And didn't they — ?

JOE. They looked at me as though I was so much air. They didn't seem to hear my voice. (*Her grasp tightens on his shoulder in speechless sympathy. As they sit so, three men pass the window; stop. The voice of one can be heard.*)

AL (*offstage*). This is the place. Come on. (JOE *and* MARY *rise and stand listening. There is a sound in the hall as the outer door of the house is opened and closed. There comes a heavy knock on the door R.C.*)

MARY. Joe! Whatever they do, don't try to stop them. Let them take the things. I couldn't stand a quarrel.

JOE. All right, Mary. It wouldn't do any good anyway. They've got the law on their side. (*The knock comes again. She answers quietly.*)

MARY. Come in. (*The* CITY MARSHAL *and his two helpers enter. The* MARSHAL *is a big slow man, of the ward politician type.* AL *is a burly fellow of about forty, ready to be belligerent if necessary.* TIM *is a young fellow in his twenties, with a friendly face.*)

MARSHAL. Lookin' fer Joseph Doe.

JOE. I'm Joseph Doe.

MARSHAL (*has been looking round and taking in* MARY *and the baby. His tone is less aggressive but still firm. He addresses* JOE.) Well, buddy, guess you know what we've come fer. (JOE *stares at him, a prey to so many conflicting emotions as to seem incapable of speech.*)

MARY. Yes, we know. Couldn't you let us stay for a few more days till we can find a place to live?

MARSHAL (*mildly, but with firmness*). You've had three months fer that, lady.

JOE. Oh, Mary! What's the use? What do they care? Go ahead and clear the place out, if you want.

(*The men set to work with a rough efficiency. The kitchen cupboard is nearest the door and they take that first. Any small things they come on they tuck swiftly into drawers and clear the way as they go.* MARY *sits in her chair, watching them with a white face.* JOE *stands near the baby's cradle. From the sounds as the men work on, it is evident that the furniture is being stacked outside in the street on the other side of the window. When everything but Mary's chair and the cradle have been cleared from the room,* AL *pushes open the door L.C., goes in and they carry out other pieces from there. The fading light outside deepens into dusk.*)

TIM (*with great civility*). 'Scuse me, could you let us have a light?

JOE (*indicating the candle on the mantel*). That's all the light we've got. The gas is turned off.

TIM. Thank ye. (*He lights the candle, carries it into the other room, returns with a battered suitcase.*) 'Scuse me, but I think you'll want this fer yer clothes.

MARY. Oh, yes! Joe, we ought to pack things.

JOE. You sit still. I'll do it. (*He goes out into the other room, returns with an armful of things, hands* MARY *her hat and coat, packs the other things quickly and carelessly into the case. The men have finished taking out the furniture from the inner room.* AL *comes out and begins to take down the curtains at the window in the right side wall.* TIM *brings the candle and sets it again on the mantel. The dusk is deepening.* JOE *comes to the baby's cloak and bonnet, which he hands to* MARY. *They work silently, with understanding nods and gestures.* MARY *is shivering, half with the cold, half from nervousness.*)

(*Again from far down the street comes the sound of the singing, drawing nearer. As both doors are now open to the street, it can be heard clearly.*)

CHORUS (*singing*).

> God rest you, merry gentlemen,
> Let nothing you dismay,
> Remember Christ, our Saviour,
> Was born on Christmas day.

MARY (*attention attracted, half by the song, half by* AL's *taking down the curtains, toward the window, sees that it is snowing down on her things piled outside*).   Joe! It's snowing!

JOE (*looking up briefly from his packing*).   Gad! So it is!

CHORUS (*singing*).

> To save poor souls from Satan's power
> Which had long time gone astray
> And it is tidings of comfort and joy.

(MARY *stands still, listening to the singing.* TIM *sees her listening and listens too.*)

TIM.   Singin'!

MARY.   It's the Sunday school children from the church down the street. They pass the window all the time.

CHORUS.

> From God that is our Father
> The blessed angels came
> Unto some certain shepherds
> With tidings of the same.

TIM.   That's right. It's Christmas Eve.

MARY.   Yes. Christmas Eve.

TIM.   Gee, lady! I wisht we didn't hev to do this ternight.

JOE (*his voice hard with bitter tension*).   Ha! Christmas Eve! So 'tis! Isn't that nice! Merry Christmas, everybody!

MARY.   Joe! Don't!

JOE.   But it's so funny! Isn't it funny? Here I almost forgot to give you that diamond tiara I bought for you! (MARY *lays her hand gently over Joe's lips. She does it so affectionately it is more of a caress than a rebuke.* AL *puts the curtains in the table drawer. He picks up Mary's chair and motions to* TIM *to take the cradle.*)

MARY (*noting the gesture, lifts the baby from the cradle and wraps it in the clothing she has laid aside for it. She has already put on her own coat and hat.*) Please! Must you put those out in the snow? (TIM *makes a friendly gesture to her to leave it to him. He picks up the cradle and follows* AL *out R.C. The room is empty.* JOE *looks for his hat, puts it on, buttons his thin coat tighter around his neck — he has no overcoat — and turns to* MARY.)

MARSHAL (*reappearing in R.C. doorway*). All right, folks. Out ye go. Where's the key to this door?

JOE. We've never had a key.

MARSHAL. No key! What do you do?

JOE. We use the bolt when we're inside. When we go out we just shut the door and take a chance.

MARSHAL (*to* TIM). I got to buy a padlock. And I ain't got no cash but my carfare. You got any money?

TIM. Not a cent, fer a padlock.

MARSHAL (*turning to* AL). Ner you? (AL *shakes his head.*) Then I got ter go back ter th' office. Gad! What do ye know about that?

TIM. How long'll you be?

MARSHAL. 'Bout twenty minutes. Half hour.

CHORUS (*from up the street, singing*).

That there was born in Bethlehem
The Son of God by name,
And it's tidings of comfort and joy.
Tidings of comfort and joy.

TIM. Can't the folks stay till you get back?

MARSHAL. Sure. Ef they want to. You kin go along home. (*Goes out R.C. and can be seen passing the window.* AL *follows him out.*)

TIM. Say, lady, I put the crib and the big chair out in a corner of the hall. They'll be dry and safe there and nobody'll notice them.

MARY. Oh, thank you. (JOE *nods his appreciation.*)

TIM (*picking up his hat and turning toward the R.C. door*). S'long. (*At the door he stops, hesitates, slips his hand in his pocket, and turns back.*)   Here, kid (*he lays a coin in the baby's hand*).

MARY.   Oh, you mustn't give him that.

TIM.   Sure.   That's fer Christmas.   G'long, lady.   I got kids of my own.   Believe me, ef I didn't have I wouldn't be doin' this dirty job.

MARY.   You are very kind.   I will tell him about it some day when he is older.   Look, Joe.

JOE.   Thanky. (*He shakes hands with* TIM *awkwardly.*)

TIM (*as he departs R.C.*).   O.k.   Better luck. (*He leaves the door open.*)

JOE.   Same to you.

MARY.   You see.   There are some kind people.

JOE.   Mighty few. (*But his eyes are shining.*)   But we got something to get some supper with, anyway.   Now we can get in some restaurant out of the wet and eat.

MARY (*smiles at him.* TIM *has cheered them both.*)   Joe, why wouldn't it be a good idea to go to the policeman up here at the corner and ask him where we can go?

JOE.   To a policeman?   Gee!   I wouldn't do that.

MARY.   Why not?

JOE.   You don't know what a copper might do to you.

MARY.   Why?   We haven't done anything wrong.

JOE.   No, of course not, but all the same he might arrest us for being vagrants or something like that.   Why, they might lock us up in a station house.   And nobody knows us here.   No! I wouldn't risk it, Mary.

MARY (*thoughtfully*).   He's always smiled at the baby when I've had him out.   But perhaps you're right.

(*The children's singing is very close.   Their voices ring out in happy ecstasy.*)

CHORUS.

God bless the ruler of this house
And send him long to reign,

And many a merry Christmas
May live to see again
Among your friends and kindred
That live both far and near.
And God send you a happy New Year,
And God send you a happy New Year.

(JOE *and* MARY *have started toward the R.C. door.* JOE *halts* MARY *by a touch on her arm.*)

JOE.   Let's wait till the kids get by. (*They stand silent together as the children start to pass the window.*)

MARY.   Joe, perhaps we could go down into the subway and stay there till morning.

JOE.   Say, that's a good idea. You could sit down there and be out of the weather. If they'll let us stay. (*The song outside breaks off abruptly. A few of the younger children trail on for a moment, then stop also.*)

SALLIE (*offstage in a clear girlish voice*).   Oh! Look at all the furniture!

CHILDREN.   Out in the street! — In the snow! — Somebody's moving in! — Somebody's moving out! — But it's getting all wet!

DICK.   I know what this means. They've been evicted!

SALLIE.   Hush! Are those the people?

DICK.   Yes. I believe they must be.

LUCY.   Shan't we sing to them?

SALLIE.   No, that wouldn't be kind. Dick, what are you going to do?

DICK.   Wait here a minute.

SALLIE.   Are you going in?

DICK.   Yes. Maybe they need help.

(*Their voices have been growing more audible as they enter the outer hallway and come to the open door R.C.* DICK *enters. He is a fine-looking boy of about fifteen, in Scout uniform.* SALLIE *is right behind him. She is perhaps fifteen, a fine wholesome girl in uniform. Behind these two the others follow in.* TED *and* ALICE *are slightly younger than the first two. The others can be any ages desired. They are none of them richly dressed but they all look like the rosy-cheeked, sweet-faced children of people in comfortable circumstances. The younger ones are shy, as children should be shy in a wholesome, modest, friendly fashion.*)

DICK (*removing his cap as he advances*).   Excuse me, sir, but is this your furniture out here?

JOE (*in a furtive aside to* MARY).   Aw, what's that his business?

MARY.   Dear! He's just a nice boy! (*Turns to* DICK *with a sweet smile.*) Yes, it is ours.

SALLIE (*who has come down on the other side of* MARY).   But it's getting all wet.

JOE (*wearily*).   We know that.

DICK.   Well, excuse me, sir. I don't want to butt in. I just thought that maybe you'd like to have Ted and me carry it somewhere out of the snow.

MARY.   You are very kind. That's kind of them, Joe.

JOE.   Yes. But the trouble is I don't know where you could take it.

DICK.   Oh! Couldn't we put it back in here for the night?

JOE.   The fellow that moved it out will be back in a few minutes. He wouldn't stand for it. You see, I can't pay my rent.

DICK.   I — I'm sorry. But perhaps we could put it in the basement of the parish house till you do know where you want it to go. That's just a step down here.

MARY.   Oh, Joe! That would be wonderful.

DICK (*turning to* TED, *who is standing near him*).   Ted! You run down and ask Mr. Chase if we can move some things into the basement.

TED.   Sure! (*He is off R.C. like a flash.*)

JOE.   Who's this Mr. Chase?

DICK.   He's the man the church appointed to run the parish house. Say, he's a prince! You ought to know him.

SALLIE (*has been standing quietly by. Now she suddenly sees something that interests her.*) Why! There's a baby! (MARY *smiles and lifts the dark shawl she has wrapped over the child so that* SALLIE *can see him.*)

ALICE (*drawing nearer to* MARY). A baby? A real live baby!

(*The little folk in the doorway suddenly surge forward. Here is something that makes them feel at home.* DICK *turns swiftly and goes out into the hall. In a moment he returns, bringing the big chair, which he sets in its old place in obedience to an unconscious gesture from* MARY.)

CHILDREN (*in a buzz of sweet, low voices*). A baby! Is he asleep? Hush! We mustn't wake him up! I want to see him! Oh, isn't he darling!

DICK. You might as well be sitting down, madam, till Ted comes back.

MARY. Thank you! (*She sits in the chair.* DICK *places the footstool for her.* JOE *nods his appreciation.*)

DICK. Do you mind the kids coming in, sir?

JOE. Not at all. (*With a sardonic smile*) It isn't *my* flat!

DICK. I don't like to let 'em stand still in the street. Though it isn't much warmer in here.

JOE. No, there isn't any heat.

MARY (*shivering visibly*). It *is* cold!

JOE (*watching her with anxiety*). You ought to have warmer clothes, Mary!

MARY (*trying to control her shivering*). I'm all right, dear. I'll get warm when we eat.

DICK (*looking at the hearth*). Why don't we make a fire?

JOE. We can only stay here for a few minutes, till the marshal gets back.

DICK. Even so. That will take him some time. And Ted may not find Mr. Chase at once. I think I'll make a little fire if you don't mind.

JOE. Right-o! But there isn't anything to burn. Unless we take a piece of furniture. We might as well.

DICK (*turning to* HAL *and* JOHN). That grocer up at the

corner was throwing out some packing boxes as we came along.

HAL.   Sure. I'll get 'em.

JOE.   I'll get them. Why should we put you chaps to any trouble?

HAL.   Gee, mister, I'm glad to do it. It'll be a good deed and I need one the worst way.

JOE.   You need one?

HAL.   Yep. Boy Scout — one a day. An' mother and dad and Aunt Kate and the church all kept me so busy runnin' errands fer the last week — (*He is quite riled over it all.*) Gee! I ain't had a chance ter do a good deed fer a coon's age. (*Belligerently*) Give a feller a chance!

JOE (*smiling, friendly*). Sure thing, old man. Go to it!

HAL.   Hot dog! C'mon, John! (*He and* JOHN, *quite cheerful again, dash out R.C.*)

ALICE (*hanging over the baby*). May I just touch him, ma'am?

MARY.   Yes. But try not to wake him, dear. (ALICE *takes the baby's hand very gently. The other little children tiptoe closer to* MARY.)

LUCY.   I could hold him for you, ma'am.

MARY.   Thank you. Don't you think he might wake up if we moved him?

LUCY (*with a very maternal air*).   No, ma'am, I never wakes my babies up.

MARY (*equally serious*). Don't you? You must be very successful with them!

LUCY.   Yes'm. I am.

MARY.   How many have you?

LUCY.   We got four at home younger than me.

MARY.   What a lovely family!

LUCY.   Yes'm, that's what everybody says. (*The little girls are clustering closer, peeping at the baby.* MARY *shivers.*)

ALICE (*draws* SALLIE *aside*). Sallie, that lady's awful cold.

Don't you think I could borrow Mary's robe for her from the church? The one in the play.

SALLIE.   Why, yes! Mrs. Pearce left it in the dressing room. She said it was a pity somebody couldn't have it because it is so warm.

ALICE.   I'll run over and ask her.

SALLIE.   That's a sweet thought of yours, Alice. You do it! (ALICE *goes out R.C.*)

LUCY (*taking charge of the group clustered around* MARY, *waves them to stand farther away and puts her finger to her lips in token of silence*). Give him air, children! And hush! You'll wake him up! (*The children stop crowding, and stand respectful and quiet, a friendly-eyed, smiling little circle.*)

(HAL *and* JOHN *return R.C. with their arms full of the kindling they have made from the boxes. One of them has a newspaper and they proceed expeditiously to lay a fire and light it.*)

JOE.   Let me move your chair nearer to it, Mary. (*She rises and he and* DICK *move the chair and footstool to L.C.*)

DICK (*in a manly way as though he and* JOE *were of the same age*). You know, half the management of kids is keepin' them moving.

JOE.   I don't doubt it. You head of the troop?

DICK.   Oh, no. Just a patrol leader.

JOE.   That's a responsibility.

DICK.   Yes, sir. A man — (*he hesitates, then says modestly*) — a chap has to watch his step.

JOE.   Taking all those children across the streets and all! It's a man's job!

DICK.   Yep! (*He brightens at being appreciated.* JOE *also has begun to relax emotionally and look more cheerful. Who could help it with this crowd? The blaze throws light and warmth over them all. The room in spite of its empty bareness has become a place of good cheer.*)

MARY (*drawing little* BOBBIE *closer to her. He is a chubby youngster of about nine.*) And are you a Scout, too?

BOBBIE.   I'm a cub.

MARY.   A cub?

DICK.   You see, madam, a boy can't be a Scout till he's twelve. But he can be a cub when he's nine.

MARY.   I see.   You're a splendid cub, I think.

BOBBIE.   I'm going on ten! And I'm going to be a Scout and a baseball fan — and a Lion!

MARY (*looking startled*).   A Lion? (*The little girls giggle.*)

BOBBIE (*looks at them indignantly*).   Yep! I am so going to be a Lion.

MARY.   And what will you do when you're a lion? Roar? And scare us all?

BOBBIE.   No, ma'am.   Not that kind of a lion.   I'm going to be a Lion like daddy.

JOE.   You mean belong to the Society of Lions? (BOBBIE *nods uncertainly. He is not very sure just what he means.*) Lot of men going out to lunches.   Looking up business for their town — and all that?

BOBBIE (*attaches himself to* JOE. *Here is an understanding soul.*)   Yes, sir.   That's the kind of a lion I mean.

JOE.   Great! You do that, son.

MARY (*to* JOHN).   And what are you going to do?

JOHN.   I'm going to run an engine.

HAL.   I'm going to be a pilot on an airplane.

JOE (*whimsically*).   Let's hear from the ladies. (*He turns to* SALLIE)   How about you?

SALLIE.   I'm going to teach school.

JOE.   Fine! We'll send the baby to your school. (*Turns to* LUCY)   And you?

LUCY.   I'm going to be a singer.   I'm in the choir in the church.

DICK.   But Lucy, you may not have a voice when you're grown up.

LUCY.   I've got a voice now.   I can yell so you can hear me for a block.

JOE. Of course she'll have a voice. (*He looks at* MAGGIE, *a little honest-looking girl with Irish eyes.*) And you, madam? What are you going to be?

MAGGIE (*sweetly, still staring entranced at the baby*). Oh, sir, I want to be — a mother!

JOE (*touched*). Good for you! That's the best answer yet! (MARY, *smiling, puts her arm around* MAGGIE *and draws her close to her.*)

(*Steps are heard outside; they turn into the hall, and* TED *enters R.C. with* MR. CHASE, *a man of early middle life, kindly, substantial, with a fine face.*)

DICK (*to* JOE). This is Mr. Chase, sir. I don't know your name.

JOE. I'm Joseph Doe. (CHASE *shakes hands with* JOE, *taking him in with a quiet, appraising glance.* JOE *introduces* MARY) My wife, Mrs. Doe. (CHASE *shakes hands with* MARY *and smiles at the baby. He nods to the children. They all know him. He turns back to* JOE.)

CHASE. Out of work, son?

JOE. For the last six months.

CHASE. What's your line?

JOE. Electrical engineer.

CHASE (*indicating the room*). Dispossessed? (JOE *hands him the paper from his pocket.* CHASE *pockets it.*) I'll take care of that. Had any plans where you were going to spend the night?

JOE. We thought they might let us stay in the subway. Till morning. It'd be dry.

CHASE. Wouldn't you rather stay here?

JOE. Of course, if the marshal would let us, but he won't.

CHASE. He will. I'll fix it. (*He turns to* DICK *and* TED) Give us a hand, boys. We'll get those things back in here.

JOE. But the marshal's coming back with a padlock. I'll just be getting you all into trouble.

CHASE. Not a bit.

JOE. The rent hasn't been paid for three months.

CHASE. The church has a fund for just such things as that.

JOE. But I don't belong to your church, Mr. Chase. I've never been there.

CHASE (*leading the way out*). Anybody that needs us belongs to us. (JOE, *inarticulate with emotion, looks at* MARY *and shakes his head at her. She smiles at him happily.*)

MARY. There *are* some kind people in this place, Joe.

JOE (*with a catch in his voice*). I'll say there are!

(*The two older boys have gone with* CHASE. JOE *follows them out R.C.* MARY *sits, starry-eyed with happiness, with the younger children about her.* HAL *and* JOHN *nod to each other and go out R.C.*)

SALLIE. May we come in sometimes after school and play with the baby?

MARY. I hope you will. He'll be getting old enough to know you. Won't that be fun?

LUCY. I'll come every day and see that he's all right.

MARY. Oh, thank you!

LUCY. This is your first baby, isn't he?

MARY. Yes.

LUCY. There'll be a lot of things you won't know about. How to feed him and all.

MARY. I do feel very inexperienced.

LUCY. I know all about how to take care of him. You can depend on me.

MARY (*with sweet gratitude*). Thank you!

(ALICE *enters with " Mary's robe." It is made of some warm-looking woolly stuff in a beautiful soft blue, the color traditional for Mary. It is ornamented with gold stenciling and trimmed with white fur at neck and sleeves.* SALLIE *and* ALICE *hold it up for* MARY *to put on.*)

ALICE. Please, ma'am, Mrs. Pearce said you could keep it. Now the play is over we haven't any use for it.

MARY. For me? That lovely thing! Oh! (*She stands up and gives the baby to* LUCY *to hold.*) Will you take him, dear, for a minute? (LUCY *takes the baby with a great air of authority.*)

(*They put the robe on* MARY *and fasten it around her with the girdle. It gives her a sudden queenly beauty. The children feel it and stare up at her with something verging upon awe.* MARY *sits again and holds out her arms for the child.* LUCY *lays it in her arms. The light from the fire throws an amber radiance on her. She is dazzlingly lovely. Meanwhile,* CHASE, JOE *and the boys have been bringing the furniture back into the rooms and placing the pieces where they belong.* SALLIE *and* ALICE *turn to and dry the furniture with a duster they have picked up, or arrange small things on top of the dresser, etc.*)

JOE (*as he and* CHASE *place the table D.C.*). I think I ought to tell you that we don't belong in this place.

CHASE. How do you mean?

JOE. We only came here six months ago. We're strangers.

CHASE (*nodding toward the children with* MARY). Call that being strangers? They look to me like old friends.

(JOE *stares at the group by the fire, gulps, grows inarticulate, shakes his head and gives up trying to explain. As he turns toward the door the* MARSHAL *enters and stands amazed, padlock in hand.*)

MARSHAL. Well, well, what's all this?

JOE (*to* CHASE). The city marshal. (CHASE *goes up to him, and they talk apart. The* MARSHAL *smiles after a moment, nods;* CHASE *takes his arm and they go out into the hall.* JOE *follows them.*)

ALICE (*to* SALLIE). Sallie, he called her **Mary** and she called him Joe. And there's the baby. It's just like our play in the church today.

LUCY. It is. Just like the play. Lady, what's the baby's name?

MARY. Christopher. Why?

SALLIE. That's like the play, too. (*The children stare, more awestruck than ever.*)

ALICE. Couldn't we sing our song to this Mary? And to this little Christopher?

SALLIE (*to* MARY). May we sing our song? You see, we've all been in a play at church. We were the angels who came to see the little Christ child. We'd like to sing to Christopher.

MARY. That would be beautiful. (*She too is moved at the thought.*)

(HAL *and* JOHN *re-enter R.C. They have a box of wood they place by the fire. They go out again.* JOE *and* CHASE *re-enter.*)

(*Ever since the entrance of the children the room has become increasingly beautiful, cheerful and homelike, and the atmosphere developed in the feeling between the Does and the children more and more intimate and affectionate. Now there creeps in a serious note, a touch of reverence on the part of the children toward* MARY *and the child. In their own minds they are back in the nativity play they have given in the church.*)

LUCY (*who has been whispering to* SALLIE, *now turns to* MARY). Please, ma'am, may we put little Chris in his crib and sing to him there? This is called the crib song, you know.

MARY. Of course, dear.

(LUCY *bustles round making the cradle ready for the baby. She takes out the pillow and shakes it up, warms the bedding at the fire and tucks it smoothly in, turns to* MARY *and holds out her arms for the child. She does all this with an air of vast experience.* MARY *puts the baby in her arms and she lays him carefully in the cradle. Under Sallie's direction — just a gesture or two — the other children, all acting their parts of little angels with great seriousness, arrange themselves around the cradle. While they are doing this,* MISS DUNCAN *enters. She wears her uniform and the beautiful Red Cross cape, dark blue with its scarlet lining. She carries a basket of Christmas dinner, piled high with bright fruit, apples and oranges on top. She and* CHASE *nod to each other. All the children know her.*)

MISS DUNCAN. Good evening, everybody.

CHILDREN. Hello, Miss Duncan! Good evening, Miss Duncan. Miss Duncan, come see the baby.

MISS DUNCAN (*to* MARY, *as she sets the basket on the table*). Good evening. This is from the church. Tomorrow's dinner, with Christmas wishes.

MARY. Oh, how wonderful! Thank you.

LUCY. Miss Duncan, see the baby!

MISS DUNCAN. That's why I came. I heard there was a baby. Is he well?

MARY. Very well. Come look at him. (*She leads* MISS DUNCAN *to the cradle.* MISS DUNCAN *holds out her hands to the baby, touching him deftly.*)

MISS DUNCAN. Oh, what a lovely little fellow!

MARY. He is to me.

MISS DUNCAN. And are you well?

MARY. Yes, very well. And so happy — with all our new friends!

(HAL *and* JOHN *come in with a little Christmas tree which they stand on the table. They also have a quantity of Christmas greens and they proceed to decorate the room with them.*)

HAL. See what the grocer gave us!

JOHN. He said it was too late to sell it and we could have it now.

MARY. And you are giving it to us?

HAL. Of course.

MARY. I think it must be the third or fourth good deed. We do thank you. (*She sees the children are waiting to sing. She sits again in her thronelike chair and motions to* MISS DUNCAN *to sit in the other chair.* JOE, *his attention attracted, comes and stands behind her, looking on. The group makes a picture suggestive of the Holy Family in the manger.*)

A SINGLE CLEAR LITTLE VOICE (*sings*).

Peace to all that have good will!
God, who heaven and earth doth fill,

Comes to turn us away from ill,
And lies so still
Within the crib of Mary.
CHORUS (*all the·children*).
He came among us at Christmastide,
At Christmastide,
In Bethlehem;
Men shall bring him from far and wide
Love's diadem:
Jesus, Jesus,
Lo, he comes, and loves, and saves, and frees us!
THE SINGLE VOICE (*sings*).
All shall come and bow the knee;
Wise and happy their souls shall be,
Loving such a divinity
As all may see
In Jesus, Son of Mary.
(*Chorus by all the children.*)
THE SINGLE VOICE (*sings*).
Thou my lazy heart hast stirred,
Thou, the Father's eternal Word,
Greater than aught that ear hath heard,
Thou tiny bird
Of love, thou Son of Mary.
(*Chorus by all the children. As the song ends the* POLICEMAN
*in uniform enters and comes down to R. of table. The children
greet him affectionately.*)
POLICEMAN (*removing his helmet with a gesture of reverence
toward the nativity group*). Sure, 'tis the picture in the
church!
CHASE. Good evening, Mack.
POLICEMAN. Evenin', sor. Sure, an' I've been wonderin'
what became of the children an' thin I heard their voices
here.
CHILDREN. Oh, there's Mack! Evenin', Mr. Mack! Eve-

nin'! (*Some of them sidle up to him, take his hands and bring him down toward* JOE *and* MARY, *nearer the fire.*)

CHASE.   We've been giving a little party for the Does.   You know Joe here?

POLICEMAN (*extending a large and kindly hand*).   Sure, seen him often.   Know everybody on me beat.

JOE (*introducing* MARY).   And my wife.

MARY.   I know you!   You've helped me across the street.

POLICEMAN.   That's nothing, lady.   (*He looks down at little* MAGGIE, *who has gone fast to sleep beside Mary's chair.*)   An' what do you know about this?   Me own little girl!   Aslape at a party!   (*He bends over her with great gentleness.*)   Maggie! Maggie, me dear!   (*She opens one eye sleepily.*)   Sure, I'll be takin' her home.   (*He gathers her up on his shoulder.*)

MARY.   Is she really your little girl?

POLICEMAN.   She is that!   An' that spalpeen (*indicating* TED) — he's after bein' mine, too.   (*He turns to all the others*) Come on, all you kids!   Yer mothers'll be lookin' fer ye!   An' blamin' me, they will, fer not runnin' ye home!

DICK.   Our mothers all know we're out singing carols, Mr. Mack.   I don't think they're worried.

POLICEMAN.   Not worried?   An' with th' traffic all going siven ways fer Sunday?   Sure, an' I know yer mothers better then ye do.

MARY.   I should be worried.

POLICEMAN.   And how!   It's me they'll be blamin'!   "What's the matter wid the cop?" they'll be sayin'.   Come along wid yez now.   I'll be seein' ye through the streets.

CHASE.   Right, Mack.   Don't know what we'd do without you. (POLICEMAN *is shepherding the children toward the R.C. door. Each as he or she passes* MARY *and* JOE *nods or smiles, drops a little courtesy.*)

CHASE (*turns to* JOE).   Come in, Joe, on Monday.   I've got a job for you.

JOE.   You mean it, sir?   A real job!

CHASE. Some electrical repairs at the church. (*He hands him a couple of bills.*) Put this in your pocket. Yes, take it! (*JOE hesitates.*) Just an advance on your wages.

JOE (*taking the money*). Thank you, sir. I never can tell you —

CHASE. I understand. Glad we got together. (*He goes out with* MISS DUNCAN.)

CHILDREN (*calling as they go out*). Good night, Mrs. Doe. Good night. Good night. I'll be coming in to see Christopher. Yes, we'll all be coming in. Good night, little Chris. (*They go out with* POLICEMAN *at their heels.* MARY *and* JOE *and baby are left alone. Outside in the street the children take up a song.*)

CHILDREN (*their voices fading slowly as they walk away*).
God rest you, merry gentlemen,
Let nothing you dismay,
For Jesus Christ, our Saviour,
Was born upon this day
To save us all from Satan's power
When we were gone astray.

(JOE *and* MARY *turn toward each other across the table. They are smiling but moved.*)

JOE. What made all those people act like that to you and me? I don't know!

MARY (*reverently*). I know! A little thing!

JOE. What?

MARY. Just a baby Christ, born in Bethlehem, twenty centuries ago!

CHILDREN (*singing at a distance*).
O tidings of comfort and joy,
Tidings of comfort and joy,
For Jesus Christ, our Saviour,
Was born on Christmas day.

(*As the song fades the curtain is lowered.*)

PAWNS*

by

Percival Wilde

CHARACTERS

ILIA — *young son boy* ⎫
GRIGOR — *father* ⎬ *Russian*
STEPAN — *older son* ⎭

MICHAEL

PETER

SERGEANT

Scene: A forest of swampy nature near the frontier between
Russia and Austria.

Time: Night — just before dawn.

PAWNS

The curtain rises in darkness. Here and there, little irregular hummocks of ground. Frogs croaking. Near the center, a small fire with a thin, straight flame casting but little light, so that ten feet away from it there is darkness.

Three men are grouped about the fire: GRIGOR, *a Russian peasant in his fifties, bearded, grave, with something of the peculiar dignity which his class acquires as it ages;* STEPAN, *his older son, enormous, powerful, bearded, stretched out full length on the ground; and the younger son,* ILIA, *hardly more than a boy.*

A pause.

ILIA. An hour more and it will be light. I can tell by the croaking of the frogs. It is as if they were afraid of the light. Their croaking is different. Listen! (*A pause.*)

GRIGOR. Thirty versts more to Zawichost. *- loveday,*

ILIA. Is it so far? That is farther than I have ever been.

GRIGOR. What of that? By nightfall we will be there.

STEPAN (*moving his huge frame lazily*). And then, God willing, one more day, and we return home!

GRIGOR. God willing!

ILIA. Is it a large city? Will there be many people?

STEPAN (*with an indulgent smile*). More than you have ever seen before.

ILIA. That will be wonderful!

STEPAN. There are streets, more streets than you can count, and shops where they sell beautiful things, and great houses all built of stone.

ILIA. I shall love to see that!

GRIGOR. Not I! (*He shakes his head.*) I am afraid of the

53

cities! Oh, I am afraid of the cities! (*He addresses* STEPAN) Had you not gone to the city, they would have left us alone.

STEPAN. No.

GRIGOR. They have always left us alone. Here are the marshes and the quicksands. Who knows his way through them? Not the city people. They are far too comfortable in their stone houses.

STEPAN. Nevertheless they would have sent for us. So the police said.

GRIGOR. The police? Since when do we talk with the police? Have I not said that when an honest moujik sees a policeman on one side of the street he crosses to the other?

STEPAN. It was no use. There were too many of them. There were police at every corner. There were signs in the street, and crowds reading the signs.

GRIGOR. Signs! Ah, yes! Signs telling you what to do! Signs telling you what not to do! But read? How should a moujik read? How to plow a straight furrow in the earth, when to sow, when to reap, how to feed his hens, his cow — that he knows, and that is far better than reading signs! Pah! Because you could not read, they told you what they pleased!

STEPAN. So I thought at first.

GRIGOR. Well?

STEPAN. Then I asked others. They all said the same.

GRIGOR. Hm! We must go to Zawichost.

STEPAN. Yes; to Zawichost.

GRIGOR. And lose three days in harvest time.

STEPAN. So they said; all of us.

GRIGOR. While Michael and lame Peter work in their field undisturbed, on the other side of the marsh! When we return, when we ask them to help us, they will refuse; we have not helped them. (*He pauses in disgust.*) If there were only a reason it would be otherwise, but for <u>mobilization</u>? (*With crowning contempt*) What *is* mobilization?

STEPAN. When I asked they pointed me out to each other;

said I was a fine hulk of a man to be asking what was mobilization. They laughed at me. They threw stones at me. (*He is
getting angry at the recollection.*) Then I took the biggest of
them by the arm — so — and I pressed a little, so that his face
went white beneath the dirt, and the sweat stood out in drops on
his forehead, and he begged for mercy, and the others, they
stopped laughing!

ILIA (*who is listening with breathless interest*).   And then?

STEPAN.   Then I came away.

(*There is a pause. Then the younger brother, who has been
much impressed, takes up the conversation.*)

ILIA.   You took him by the arm?

STEPAN (*smiling*).   Yes, little brother.

ILIA.   With one hand only?

STEPAN.   This selfsame hand. (*The boy feels the horny palm
with interest.*)   Shall I show you?

ILIA (*darting out of his reach*).   No, no! I do not doubt you!

STEPAN (*laughing*).   For that, thanks!

ILIA.   Still, if you must show me —

STEPAN (*with the growl of a good-natured bear*).   What?

ILIA.   Wait until we come to the city today.

STEPAN.   And then?

ILIA.   Perhaps they will laugh at us —

STEPAN (*with understanding*).   Yes, little brother!

ILIA.   Oh, I hope I shall see that! (*There is a pause.*)

GRIGOR.   For fifty years I have been a good Christian. I
know every holiday of the Orthodox Church. But mobilization?
That I have never heard of.

STEPAN.   Perhaps the Metropolitan has decreed a new festival.

GRIGOR.   In harvest time? Pah!

STEPAN.   Harvest time is nothing to the people who live in
cities. They know nothing of harvests.

ILIA (*suddenly*).   I hear steps.

GRIGOR.   What?

ILIA.   Listen! (*They listen.   There is no sound.*)

GRIGOR.   I hear nothing.

STEPAN.   The boy has quicker ears than you or I.   Listen. (*Still there is no sound.*)

STEPAN (*addressing* ILIA).   What do you hear?

ILIA.   Two men.

STEPAN.   Which way?

ILIA.   From there. (*He points toward R.*)

GRIGOR.   But who should come that way?   That is the way we have come.   The city is in the other direction. (*A crackling of branches becomes audible.*)

STEPAN.   Now I hear them!   Hullo!   Hullo!

VOICES.   Hullo!   Hullo!

ILIA.   Michael and lame Peter.   I know their voices.

STEPAN.   Hullo!   This way!

GRIGOR.   They will not know where we are.   Guide them. (STEPAN *starts off.*)

ILIA.   Here!   A burning fagot!

STEPAN.   Since when do I need a light, little brother? (*He disappears.*)

GRIGOR.   Michael and lame Peter?   Are you sure?

ILIA (*listening*).   I hear them speaking. . . . Now he has found them. . . . They are coming this way.

GRIGOR.   Why should they follow us?

(STEPAN *reappears, followed by two more peasants who carry packs:* PETER, *a farmhand of twenty-two, who walks with a pronounced limp; and* MICHAEL, *his employer, a robust man near Grigor's age.*)

GRIGOR (*rising ceremoniously*).   Christ be with you!

MICHAEL.   Grigor Ignátievitch, Christ be with you!

GRIGOR (*as the others drop their packs and draw near to the fire*).   What brings you to the swamp at this time of night?

MICHAEL.   We asked at the farm.   They said you had gone this way.

PETER. We too, we go to the mobilization.

GRIGOR. You also?

ILIA. You go to Zawichost?

PETER. No; to Sandomierz.

GRIGOR. Oh! So there is mobilization in more than one place at once?

ILIA. It must be a great festival indeed.

PETER (*eagerly*). A festival is it then?

GRIGOR. Who knows?

MICHAEL. But that is why we followed you. We do not know what mobilization may be. But Anna Petrovna said you had gone there. We thought you would know.

GRIGOR (*shrugging his shoulders*). Whatever it is, we will know today.

PETER. But now you cannot tell us?

GRIGOR. No. (*He pauses.*) Why do you go to the mobilization in Sandomierz while we go to that in Zawichost?

MICHAEL. A soldier said we were to go to Sandomierz.

STEPAN. A soldier here? In these swamps?

MICHAEL. All the way to the farm he came. We must go, he said. We were afraid to disobey.

GRIGOR. He did not tell you why you must go?

MICHAEL. He had no time. He had to tell many others.

STEPAN. And you asked him nothing?

MICHAEL. We asked. He swore and said that if we were not gone when he passed again on his way back, we should be beaten. (*There is a pause.*)

ILIA. And lame Peter, must he go too?

MICHAEL. I and all my men, he said. I have only the one.

ILIA. But he is lame.

PETER (*good-naturedly*). Lame Peter will travel as far and as fast as any of them! And if there is to be a festival, why should not lame Peter be there with the others?

GRIGOR. But the harvest?

MICHAEL. Yes, the harvest!

STEPAN. When we return we will reap our fields together, and then lame Peter will have a chance to show what a worker he is!

ILIA (*abruptly*). A sound! (*They stop talking.*)

STEPAN. What is it?

ILIA (*listening*). A horse.

STEPAN (*incredulously*). A horse? This time you are wrong!

GRIGOR. What fool would try to ride a horse through the swamp?

ILIA. Now I hear it more plainly.

PETER. Perhaps it is a riderless horse.

ILIA. No. A rider is using the whip. (*He is looking off L.*)

GRIGOR (*following his glance*). A rider from the city? (*The peasants look at one another. The crackling of branches becomes audible.* STEPAN *rises silently, and goes out L.*)

MICHAEL. As if there were no better use for a good animal than that! To ride through the swamp, where the ground is hardly firm enough to carry a man!

PETER. And quicksands, quicksands to right and left of him! The horse knows better than his master. (*There is the sound of a drunken voice raised in anger.*)

ILIA. Listen to him!

PETER. Swearing at his horse, as if the poor beast could do any more!

ILIA. He's afraid! I know he's afraid! He feels the earth crumbling under his hoofs! How he must tremble! (*The sound of a whip being used unmercifully.*)

ILIA. Now he's beating him! I hope he throws him! Oh, I hope he throws him! (*There is a loud crash.*)

GRIGOR. He *has* thrown him!

ILIA. I knew he would!

PETER. It serves him right! To treat a good horse like that!

ILIA.   And into the mud! The rider from the city in the mud!
I should love to see that! (*There is the report of a revolver.
The peasants rise, look at one another in terrified inquiry.*)

GRIGOR.   What was that?

MICHAEL.   A shot!

ILIA.   And Stepan!

PETER.   Perhaps Stepan said something!

ILIA.   Something the rider didn't like!

MICHAEL.   He was always quick tempered, your Stepan. He
was not the man to stand there and see the horse beaten for no
fault of its own.

GRIGOR (*in horror*).   Christ!

(STEPAN *re-enters.*)

ILIA (*with a shout of relief*).   Here he comes!

GRIGOR.   Stepan!

MICHAEL.   What happened?

STEPAN (*briefly*).   His horse fell. It wouldn't rise again.
He shot it.

ILIA.   Oh!

PETER.   Shot his horse! (*At L. there enters a Russian* SER-
GEANT, *booted, spurred, carrying a whip. He is very muddy and
very drunk.*)

PETER (*repeats in horror*).   He shot his horse!

SERGEANT.   Well, what of it? It was *my* horse, wasn't it?
I could do what I wanted with it.

MICHAEL (*more mildly*).   It must have been worth many
rubles.

SERGEANT.   The rich government will pay for it. (*He stumbles nearer the fire.*) Give me something to drink.

MICHAEL.   What would we be doing with drink?

GRIGOR.   We are only honest moujiks.

SERGEANT.   You have nothing? Well, then — (*He pulls a
flask from a pocket, and applies it to his lips.*)

STEPAN (*to* GRIGOR, *as the* SERGEANT *drinks*).   He has had
too much to drink already.

GRIGOR (*shrugging his shoulders*). A Christian is a Christian.

SERGEANT (*wiping his lips on his sleeve, and replacing his bottle without offering it elsewhere*). Ah! That puts the heart in you! Make place for me at your fire, you! (*He elbows his way to a seat. The peasants edge away so that he is alone at one side and they together at the other.*) There! That's something like. (*There is a pause.*)

GRIGOR (*courteously*). May I ask your name?

SERGEANT (*warming his hands at the fire*). What?

GRIGOR. Your name and surnames?

SERGEANT. Alexei Ivanovitch Liboff, sergeant.

GRIGOR (*inclining his head*). I am Grigor Ignátievitch Arshin. This is my son Stepan. This is my son Ilia. This is my good neighbor —

SERGEANT (*interrupts rudely with a drinking song*).

It isn't sleep that bows my head,
But the drink, the drink that's in it!

GRIGOR (*in amazement*). What?

STEPAN (*starting to rise angrily*). The boor!

GRIGOR (*laying a hand on his arm*). A Christian is a Christian.

SERGEANT.

I'll up and away to a distant glade
Where the wild red raspberries grow,
And I'll meet a little Cossack girl,
A little Cossack girl from the Don!

(*He stops suddenly.*) Well, why don't you say something?

GRIGOR. It is not for us to speak in the presence of your excellency.

SERGEANT. Then my excellency graciously grants you permission. (*He rises, bows grotesquely, stumbles, falls.*)

I'll meet a little Cossack girl,
A little Cossack girl from the Don!

(*He stops, points at* ILIA.) You, speak! (ILIA *remains silent.*

He points at STEPAN.) You! (STEPAN *folds his arms and glares. He points at* GRIGOR.) You, old man! Are you all a pack of fools?

GRIGOR. Your excellency has traveled far?

SERGEANT. My excellency has traveled far. Through these cursed swamps on a stumbling horse all the way from Zawichost.

STEPAN (*involuntarily*). From Zawichost?

SERGEANT. Have I not said so? All the way from Zawichost, since eleven o'clock this morning.

STEPAN (*starting to put the question which is uppermost in all their minds*). Perhaps, then — (*He breaks off.*)

SERGEANT. Perhaps what?

GRIGOR. Perhaps your excellency can tell us something of the mobilization?

SERGEANT (*yawning*). The mobilization, oh, yes.

ILIA. It is a festival, is it not?

SERGEANT (*shutting his mouth with a surprised snap*). What?

GRIGOR. A festival of the holy church?

SERGEANT. Who told you that? (*He laughs loudly.*) A festival of the church!

MICHAEL (*somewhat nettled*). What, then, is the mobilization?

SERGEANT. You don't know?

PETER. How should we? We live far from the cities.

SERGEANT. Then why do you go there?

MICHAEL. We do as we are told.

SERGEANT (*very drunkenly*). Quite right! Do as you are told! Obey orders! That's the way for a moujik!

GRIGOR. But what is mobilization?

SERGEANT (*turning on him*). Mobilization is this: they stand you up in rows, the big men in back, and the little men in front. Then they put guns in your hands, and you shoot.

ILIA. I should love to shoot.

MICHAEL. But we don't know how.

SERGEANT. That doesn't matter. They teach you.

STEPAN. We shoot. Very well, what then? When we have shot do we go home?

SERGEANT. Oh, no! It only begins so. When you have shot, you march. Then they stand you up in rows again, and you shoot some more.

MICHAEL. What do you shoot at?

ILIA. Targets?

SERGEANT. Better than that!

PETER. Animals?

SERGEANT. Still better than that! (*He pauses for his effect.*) How would you like to shoot at men?

ILIA. Shoot at men?

MICHAEL. What have they done that they should be shot at?

GRIGOR. What have we done that we should shoot at them?

SERGEANT (*amused*). You don't believe me? (*He laughs, produces his bottle, drinks again.*)

STEPAN (*to* GRIGOR). He is very drunk. He doesn't know what he is saying.

PETER (*with a sudden laugh*). I have found it!

SERGEANT. What have you found?

PETER. I have found the trick! You shoot at men, yes, but not with real bullets!

SERGEANT (*laughing, as the others laugh, but for a different reason*). Not with real bullets? Wait a minute. (*He fumbles in his bandolier.*) Here's one of them! (*He tosses them a loaded cartridge.*)

MICHAEL (*while they all examine it with curiosity*). What is it?

SERGEANT. Give it to me. (*He demonstrates*) This is full of powder. The hammer strikes here, and the powder explodes. And this — this (*he bites it out*) — is the bullet. (*He passes it to them.*)

ILIA. What a cruel thing!

PETER. How heavy it is!

GRIGOR. And is this what we shoot at men?

SERGEANT. Bullets like this — and bigger.

GRIGOR. But if we hit them?

SERGEANT. What?

GRIGOR (*repeating his question*). If we hit them?

SERGEANT. You want to hit them.

GRIGOR. And hurt them?

SERGEANT. You want to hurt them.

GRIGOR. Or even — kill them?

SERGEANT (*reaching his climax*). You want to kill them!

(*The peasants look at one another blankly. The* SERGEANT *is immensely pleased with the impression he has produced.*)

STEPAN. We are peaceable moujiks.

MICHAEL. We want to kill nobody.

PETER. They must have sent for the wrong men. They could not have wanted us.

GRIGOR (*voicing the general opinion*). We, we want to kill no man. For fifty years I have been a good Christian. I have killed nothing except that which I was to eat — I and my children. We do not eat men; we do not kill men.

SERGEANT. All right, then. You will learn how.

GRIGOR. I do not wish to learn how.

SERGEANT. So they say in the beginning. So was I in the beginning. The first time you pull your trigger, the first time you see a strong man fall, you are afraid, oh, you are afraid! But then the lust of killing sweeps over you, and you shoot, and shoot, while the metal of your gun burns the flesh of your hands, and you scream with joy, and are glad, and you kill! You kill!

GRIGOR. Far rather would I be killed myself!

SERGEANT. That may happen also! (*He drinks.*)

STEPAN (*to* GRIGOR). He lies.

MICHAEL. He is a soldier. Soldiers always lie.

ILIA. And he is drunk! Pah!

GRIGOR (*to the* SERGEANT, *as he corks his bottle*). These men, whom we shoot at — (*He stops.*)

SERGEANT. Yes?

GRIGOR. They have stolen? They have murdered? (*The* SERGEANT *laughs.* GRIGOR, *patiently*) They must be great criminals. What crime have they done?

SERGEANT. No crime.

GRIGOR. Then why do they let us shoot at them?

SERGEANT. They do not *let* you.

GRIGOR. No?

SERGEANT. You shoot.

GRIGOR. And what do they do?

SERGEANT. They shoot also.

GRIGOR. At us?

SERGEANT. Where else, then? They are the enemy.

GRIGOR. But we, we have no enemy.

SERGEANT. You will learn otherwise. These men, these men whom you shoot at and who shoot at you, they are your enemy. (*There is a pause. The peasants exchange signs of incredulity.*)

ILIA (*reflectively*). To shoot, that is not so bad. But to be shot at, that I should not like at all!

GRIGOR (*silencing him*). And who are these men?

PETER (*sarcastically*). Yes, our enemies, who are they?

SERGEANT (*waving his hand*). Prussians. Germans. Austrians.

GRIGOR. And what are Prussians? — Germans? — Austrians?

SERGEANT. Men who live on the other side of the border. Men who live on the other side of the swamps.

GRIGOR. On the other side of the swamps? (*He glances meaningly at* MICHAEL *and* PETER.) What do you mean?

SERGEANT (*growing drunkenly expansive*). Well, you see, here is Russia (*a gesture L.*), here are the swamps (*a gesture in front*), that is, the border, and there is Austria. (*A gesture R.*) Here we are. There is the enemy. (*Rather unaccountably the peasants begin to laugh, a hearty laugh of relief, as if the* SERGEANT *has finally exposed the falsehood of everything that he has said by venturing upon a glaringly untrue statement.*)

SERGEANT (*irritated*). Well, what are you laughing at?

MICHAEL. A good joke!

PETER. Yes, a fine joke!

MICHAEL. A liar! Such a liar as there never was!

STEPAN. When a man has had too much to drink he should stay home!

GRIGOR (*relaxing his dignity*). And for a time we believed him! We believed him!

SERGEANT. What?

STEPAN. Instead of telling lies to honest moujiks —

SERGEANT (*interrupting*). What do you mean?

PETER. We (*indicating* MICHAEL), we live on the other side of the swamps!

SERGEANT. Well, what of it?

MICHAEL. We are going to the mobilization also!

SERGEANT (*with superiority*). Here is the border line. But the line bends.

PETER. You said they shot at us! Because we lived on the other side of the swamps! Old Grigor, and Stepan, and Ilia! They shoot at us!

STEPAN (*laughing*). Rather would we shoot at you, Alexei Ivanovitch!

SERGEANT (*growing angry*). Laugh, if you like! Laugh, but tomorrow, when you reach Zawichost, when you find that I am your superior officer, then *I* laugh!

PETER. To Zawichost? But we do not go there!

MICHAEL. We go to Sandomierz!

SERGEANT (*thunderstruck*). To Sandomierz!

PETER (*snapping his fingers at him*). Where you are *not* my superior officer!

SERGEANT (*with sudden awakening*). No, that I am not! But you, you are the enemy!

PETER. What?

ILIA. Did you hear what he said?

STEPAN (*laughing scornfully*). The enemy?

MICHAEL. When we have tilled our fields together?

SERGEANT (*balancing himself with difficulty*). Sandomierz, that is in Austria!

GRIGOR (*disregarding him*). Enemies! When we live a single verst apart from each other!

MICHAEL. When we have helped each other with the harvest, aye, since we were children!

SERGEANT (*shouting*). We are Russians! You are Austrians! There is war between us! (*He draws his revolver.*) I command you to surrender.

PETER (*mimicking him, dancing up and down in front of him*). I command you to surrender!

SERGEANT. Surrender!

PETER. Listen to the drunken fool! Surrender! (*The SERGEANT shoots. PETER falls. There is a sudden and dreadful pause.*)

STEPAN (*laying his hand over Peter's heart*). Dead! Dead as his horse!

GRIGOR (*rising to his feet like a prophet of old*). Are we men or are we beasts of the field?

SERGEANT (*turning triumphantly on MICHAEL*). Now, you Austrian swine, will you surrender? (*But STEPAN is already advancing upon him, breathing deep, slowly, massively, like some awful engine of destruction. At first the SERGEANT does not see him, but something in the expression of the others warns him. He wheels.*)

SERGEANT. Back! Stop where you are! (*STEPAN continues grimly, his great hands rising slowly from his sides.*)

SERGEANT (*in an ecstasy of fear*). Back, I say! (*He fires. STEPAN shakes himself, as if stung by a hornet, and throws his towering bulk upon the SERGEANT. There is a sigh of satisfaction from the MOUJIK as his fingers lock about his adversary's throat. And there is a scream from the SERGEANT, a scream ending in a choke. . . . The struggling figures fall outside of the circle of light. For a moment there is a threshing, as when some small animal is caught in a trap. Then quiet.)*

GRIGOR (*almost sobbing*). And not so long ago I thought it was easier to be killed than to kill!

MICHAEL (*with staring eyes*). Murder! That I have lived to see a murder!

ILIA. Lame Peter! Poor lame Peter!

(*There is a pause. Then* STEPAN *rises, holding the sergeant's revolver between two fingers.*)

STEPAN. What shall I do with this?

GRIGOR (*raising his head*). What? (STEPAN *hands him the revolver.*) Pah! (*He flings it away. A pause.*)

ILIA (*in a trembling voice*). I so wanted to see you use your strength, and now that I have seen it — how horrible it is, how horrible! (STEPAN *does not reply. Instead, he turns to* GRIGOR.)

STEPAN. The bodies?

GRIGOR. The swamp will swallow them up. (STEPAN *beckons to* ILIA. *Silently they raise Peter's body, carry it out at the back. They return.*)

GRIGOR (*rises, bows his head, folds his hands. The others follow his example.*) May we all be happy. May the dead reach God's kingdom. May we all be preserved in good health. Amen. (*The others repeat the amen. He makes the sign of the cross. The others follow his example. A little light begins to filter through the trees.*)

GRIGOR (*turning to* MICHAEL). And now, you on your way, we on ours.

MICHAEL. Farewell, brother.

GRIGOR. Brother, farewell!

(MICHAEL *takes up two packs, his own and Peter's, and goes out at the back.* GRIGOR, STEPAN, ILIA *take up their own packs, and go out L.*)

CURTAIN

HE CAME SEEING*

by

Mary P. Hamlin

CHARACTERS

ASA, *a servant*
JOAB, *his son, born blind*
HILKIAH, *a Jewish aristocrat*
JUDITH, *wife of Asa*
ANNA, *a friend of Judith*
NEIGHBORS

Scene: A room in a small stone (or mud-brick) house in Jerusalem.

Time: A morning in December, the last year of Jesus' life.

HE CAME SEEING

In back wall are two long narrow slits for windows. There is no glass, but heavy shutters drawn back against the wall show manner of closing. Center: brazier on floor. Upper right, an outside door. Near it, on back wall, is a rough wooden rack holding several pottery water jars. There is a shelf on the left wall, holding a few crude cooking utensils, including a copper bowl highly polished. Left center, a low, homemade bench; a roll of rugs in left corner and a small wooden stool, right.

As the curtain rises ASA *is seen standing, somewhat impatiently, by the door. Down center,* JOAB *stands with bent patience, enduring the many fussy little arrangements that* JUDITH *is making to his clothes. She flings his heavy cloak over one shoulder, drawing it tight about his neck. She fusses and pats and loves him, treating him like a little child.* JOAB *stands meek and willing, accustomed to it and liking it. He has never waited upon himself. He has a staff in his hand and when he moves he gropes his way, feeling timidly with the staff.*

JUDITH (*with a final unnecessary pat, and speaking with exaggerated cheer*). Careful, son.

JOAB (*listlessly*). Yes, mother.

ASA (*sharply*). Come.

JOAB. Yes, father. (*He begins to grope his way.*)

JUDITH (*with another pat to cloak*). Watch him, Asa. (*To* JOAB) You'll stay right where father puts you? (*bright, forced cheerfulness as if to a child.*)

JOAB. Yes, mother.

JUDITH. I'll come at noon and we'll take a *nice* walk about the temple porch.

JOAB. Yes, mother. (ASA *takes* JOAB *firmly by the arm and they turn to go.* JUDITH *stands watching them sadly, shaking her head in pity.*)

(*Enter* ANNA, *U.R., nodding to* ASA *and slipping by* JOAB *without his noticing her as she flattens herself against the wall to let them pass.*)

JUDITH (*with a little cry*). Wait! Your barley cakes! (*She runs up and takes from shelf three little flat cakes. These she hands to* JOAB.)

JOAB (*standing inert and speaking in disappointed tone*). Won't you bring them *hot?*

JUDITH. It's Sabbath.

JOAB (*sighing*). Oh, I forgot. (*He feels way with staff, cakes in hand.*)

JUDITH (*running to him, taking cakes and slipping them in his girdle*). You mustn't *carry* them. That's doing work.

JOAB (*patiently*). I forgot.

ASA. Mustn't forget to keep Sabbath holy, son.

JOAB. No, sir. (ASA *and* JOAB *go out U.R.*)

ANNA. Poor boy! If there's anything I hate it's stale bread.

JUDITH. I always bake it fresh other days, but I can't bake on Sabbath, can I?

ANNA (*giving* JUDITH *an appraising look, then speaking with sudden daring*). I did, once.

JUDITH (*shocked but interested*). Oh, Anna!

ANNA. Well, I forgot all about making bread the night before.

JUDITH. How *could* you?

ANNA. I don't know, but I did; so Sabbath morning I made some nice hot cakes and *nothing happened.* (*She looks defiantly at* JUDITH, *lips pursed, head held back.*)

JUDITH. It was a sin. You should have gone *without.*

ANNA. I won't let my family starve for *any*body.

JUDITH (*clapping hand over mouth in fascinated horror*). Ohhh! (*She looks at* ANNA *and they stand like children discus-*

sing delicious, forbidden things. JUDITH *clutches* ANNA *and pulls her confidentially down on bench, speaking in a scared whisper*) Anna, did you ever forget to tithe? (*She watches her friend eagerly.* ANNA *shuts lips tight, looks at* JUDITH *out of corner of eye, then with wicked joy she rocks herself back and forth and nods her head up and down.*) So did I — once.

ANNA. Anything happen to you?

JUDITH. Not a thing.

ANNA. Well, then! Judith, will you promise never to tell as long as you live? (JUDITH *nods with passionate interest.*) Swear by your head.

JUDITH (*placing hand solemnly on headband*). By my head.

ANNA (*bragging*). I don't tithe half the time.

JUDITH (*shocked squeal*). Anna!

ANNA. Hasn't anything happened — *yet.*

JUDITH (*admiring but frightened whisper*). How'd you dare?

ANNA (*with zest*). Well, once I went to market to get some mint and cummin for a lamb stew. I was so excited about having meat — it was my Thomas' birthday — I forgot to tithe the spices. I never *once* thought of it till after I was just going to sleep that night. I was scared all night long, expecting — (JUDITH *catches her lower lip in her teeth in understanding terror*) — but *nothing happened.* And then, I tried it again, on purpose, and nothing has *ever* happened; so now I just don't bother about tithing spices and little things.

JUDITH (*shocked into realizing the enormity of the offense*). And you call yourself a Pharisee?

ANNA. Of course I'm a Pharisee.

JUDITH (*jumping up and facing* ANNA *accusingly*). Not if you don't keep the law.

ANNA (*less certain*). Well, I have enough to do with all my housework, weaving and cooking and toting water for my family, without bothering to mess with every little bit of spice I use.

JUDITH. Then you aren't a Pharisee. That's all.

ANNA (*scared and savage*). I am too a Pharisee. I guess I'm own third cousin to Prince Caiaphas; and don't we eat Passover at the palace every single year?

JUDITH (*in an outburst of self-pity*). Then it isn't *fair*. Here I keep the law just the best I know how, and I have a blind baby that has to grow up a beggar, and you don't even *tithe*, and your baby's all right, and you're invited to the high priest's palace for Passover.

ANNA (*bursting to tell her news*). Judith, will you promise *never* to tell *any*body, if I tell you something?

JUDITH (*with a quick shift from reproof to curiosity*). Not a soul.

ANNA (*gloating with her news*). Well, last year when we went to the palace I kept my eyes open. You know, of course, we don't eat in the big room with the prince and his grand friends because we're poor, and we're only third cousins anyway, so we always eat in the court, near the kitchens; and I got talking with one of the scullery girls — after — and — Judith, you won't tell, because I promised on my head I wouldn't — but they don't tithe, up there, the way they tell us. *Not in the high priest's kitchens*, they don't. And what's more, Prince Caiaphas knows and doesn't say a word.

JUDITH (*genuinely shocked*). Isn't that *awful?*

ANNA. I could tell you worse'n that.

JUDITH (*eagerly*). Go on.

ANNA. There's all kinds of parties up there at the palace, with Roman officers and things not lawful (*eyes round with delicious horror*).

JUDITH (*sudden reaction, realizing that they are going too far*). We ought not to talk like this. Asa says it's our place to respect our betters. He's confidential servant to Hilkiah, the best known Pharisee in Jerusalem, and there's things *he* knows (*bragging*) — I could tell *you*, but I won't.

ANNA (*in an agony of curiosity*). Oh, *do*.

JUDITH (*struggling between temptation to show off and fear of her husband*). I don't dare. Asa'd find out. But *I* know things in high places — (*She purses lips and is aggravating.*)

ANNA. Oh, *please* tell.

JUDITH (*trembling on the verge, but pulling herself together*). I don't dare. (ANNA *clutches, pleading.*) No. (*She shakes her off.*) I can't. (*Her mind reverts to her wrongs.*) What I don't understand is why God made my baby blind.

ANNA (*glibly*). Sin.

JUDITH. What have *I* ever done?

ANNA. You must have done *something* — you or Asa or Joab.

JUDITH (*sullen*). I keep the law better'n you.

ANNA. You do now — yes — but probably you were a great sinner in a former life, Judith. Anyway, the wrath of Jehovah is upon you. You can see that.

JUDITH (*sighing*). Yes. Well, I keep the law the best I can, and so does Asa, and we've brought Joab up strict. He never does anything wrong.

ANNA (*frowning*). No, he's blind.

(*As always when women gossip, the air becomes tense. Each strives to know the most and each is annoyed with the other for keeping back possible news. They are almost on the verge of a quarrel.*)

JUDITH. Well, you needn't tell me that. I know he's blind. Just because you have a son that's all right, you needn't be so mean. I guess if you had to tend your boy, year after year, the way I do — never a free minute —

ANNA (*thinking of her own troubles*). You tend him too much. He could do more for himself if you'd let him. *Everybody* says so.

JUDITH. Oh, they do, do they? Well, then, everybody can mind their own business. I don't happen to want my boy to wait on himself. I *want* him to depend on me for *everything*.

ANNA (*sullen*). Yes, that's what every mother wants. Blindness isn't the worst trouble in this world.

JUDITH (*defiant*). What's worse?

ANNA (*bitter*). Losing your son.

JUDITH (*too self-centered to understand*). Oh, yes, I couldn't do without Joab. I'd die if I lost him.

ANNA. No, you wouldn't. You'd go right on living, same as always, only the heart inside you would be broken.

JUDITH (*in panic*). You think Joab looks sick? What you scaring me about his dying?

ANNA. Who said anything about dying? There's ways of losing besides dying.

JUDITH (*shocked out of her own sorrow by Anna's bitter tone*). Anna! What do you mean? Is it your Thomas? (ANNA *nods grimly with tight lips.*) What?

ANNA (*bursting with pent-up suffering*). Judith, I've lost him. He's *gone*. I gotta tell someone.

JUDITH (*in scared whisper*). When?

ANNA. Oh, I don't mean *that*. He comes home nights, but he's different. I have worn my fingers to the bone for that boy, Judith, and he don't pay any more attention to me than if I wasn't around. Nights he sits by the brazier and don't speak. If his father asks him a question, likely he don't even hear.

JUDITH. Perhaps he's sick.

ANNA. No. I almost wish he was, then I could nurse him and he'd need me, same as your boy needs you. That's what hurts so — he's through needing me. He won't even tell me what he's thinking.

JUDITH. Why don't you ask?

ANNA. I have, but it's worse when he talks — he says such things. His father gets so angry — angry — I've tried to reason with him, but now he don't talk at all and he don't want to hear a thing I have to say. Oh, dear, I love my boy so, but if I was *dead*, he wouldn't care.

JUDITH. Hush, Anna! That don't sound like your Thomas. I think it's only because he's growing up. They say boys are like that (*sadly*) — boys who can see.

ANNA. Oh, it's more than that. Something's troubling him,

but he won't ask our advice. He used to be such a hand to ask questions. Remember?

JUDITH (*with a quick laugh remembering the child*). Yes — "*Why?*"

ANNA. Oh, my sakes! It was "why," "why," "why," from morning to night. I used to be about crazy with him. I'd say we must be getting ready for Sabbath, and he'd say, "*Why?*" I'd say because it was the law, and he'd say *why* was it the law? I'd say, "Because Moses said so." He'd say, "*Why* did Moses say so?" I'd say, "Because Jehovah told him to," and he'd say, "*Why* did Jehovah tell him to?" And so on and so on, but now (*she throws up her hands*) — he don't ask any more. He don't care what we think. It was that very thing made his father so provoked, one night, when he did talk.

JUDITH. About Sabbath?

ANNA. Yes, he said it was silly to bother keeping Sabbath the way we do. He said God didn't *care* — said — wait till I think. It was so queer what he said — Oh, yes. "The Sabbath was made for man, not man for the Sabbath."

JUDITH (*proud that she understands*). *I* know what's the matter with him. He's been hearing that fellow from Nazareth talk. That's one of the very things it's been reported he said.

ANNA. Reported? What you mean?

JUDITH. I ought not to tell. I promised Asa I wouldn't, but you should know. He's a dangerous man. Our young men are following him. He's heading a revolution and my husband's master, Hilkiah, and some others of our leading men, they've got *spies*, and they're going to arrest him before the Romans. (*Claps hand over mouth.*) Oh, don't you ever tell I told, Anna. Asa'd be that provoked, because it's a great secret, but they know every single person that's listening to him. You must stop your Thomas.

ANNA (*clutching* JUDITH). What shall I do? (*The two women stand staring at each other in terror as* ASA *enters U.R. He looks suspiciously at them, noticing their alarm.*)

JUDITH.   Asa, Anna's Thomas is hearing that man from Galilee talk.

ASA (*sharp suspicion*).   You haven't been telling her?

JUDITH.   No, sir, I haven't told a thing, only —

ASA (*to* ANNA).   How do you know he is?

ANNA.   I don't know, Asa, only he's changed, my Thomas is, and he says things that scare me.

ASA.   What?

ANNA.   Well, one night — now, you won't ever repeat this if I tell you?

ASA.   Go on.

ANNA.   He and his father were disputing and his father backed up his side by quoting Moses, and Thomas said that Moses had been dead a long time, and, anyway, he didn't know all there was to know, and that there was newer ideas —

ASA.   The very thing that carpenter said to my master. " Moses says so and so, but *I* say — " (*The women gasp in horror.*)   Now, Anna, you mustn't repeat a word of what I tell you, but the leading Pharisees are after this fellow. He's bad. The way I know was taking in the wine.   There was supper at my master's last night and all the slaves were sent out — after — only I had to take in wine — keep it cool and take it in — so I couldn't help hearing.   But my master knows he can trust me. (*Sharply*) You won't tell? (*Both women shake heads vigorously, looking at him with scared eyes.*)   If the Romans suspect another revolution, it's all up with our people.   The fellow hails from a little mountain town and he's the most ignorant, brazen —   Why, the other day he called King Herod a *fox!* Publicly!   Said to some leading citizens, " Go, tell that fox." Fox, to the Roman governor !   What do you think of that?

ANNA.   Oh, I don't believe my boy's listening to a man like that.

ASA.   Well, if he is, you want to stop him and stop him quick.

ANNA.   Easier said than done.   Your Joab does what you tell him to, but Thomas — Oh, well, I just don't believe he's listening to a bad man. He wouldn't.

ASA. You'd be surprised the people who do listen; decent people, some of them; though most are a pretty bad lot. You must be silent about this if I tell you, but the other day he had a crowd — slaves, publicans and prostitutes — and he was stirring up that rabble to believe that Jehovah took an interest in them. He claims to know all about God, and he told them that there wasn't so much as a tail-feather on a sparrow that God didn't care about. As my master said, "You can't let *that* kind of talk go on."

ANNA *and* JUDITH (*shocked*). Oh!

ASA. He's crazy, of course; but he's dangerous. I'd rather see *my* boy dead at my feet than listening to a fellow like that.

JUDITH. Oh, Joab wouldn't listen.

ASA. Well, he can't, thank God. He can't run about after rebels.

JUDITH. No, blind but *safe*.

(*Noise of crowd outside door. Enter* JOAB, *U.R., followed by a crowd of neighbors made up of men, women and children. His entire appearance has changed. His head is up, his face radiant, as well as wet. His hair is also wet, and when he opens his outer cloak his clothes are seen to be wet and clinging. The most startling thing, however, is that his eyes are open and it is evident that he can see. He looks eagerly from* ANNA *to* JUDITH.)

JOAB. Mother! *Which?* (*He runs to* ANNA, *feels her up and down eagerly, shakes his head. Goes to* JUDITH, *feels her, then gives a glad cry*) Mother! (*He kisses her on both cheeks and holds her off by the shoulders, looking deep into her eyes.*) I said: "I will not look, I will not *see* till I have seen my mother's face. That must be first." Oh, you are *beautiful*, but your eyes are sad. I thought they would be happy eyes. Oh, my mother, how I love you! (*He runs his fingers lightly down her arms and laughs with infectious gaiety, in which the children join.*) Isn't it funny? I see you with my eyes, now, and yet to be *sure* you are my mother, I must *feel*. (*Suddenly he skips up and lifts copper bowl from shelf, his face illumined with happiness.*) Oh, this is the bowl we eat out of! *Wonderful!* (*He holds it aloft in an ecstasy of admiration.*) It is? (*He nods for confirmation to his mother.*) It is the one I have always helped you polish. You said it must be kept shining, but oh, my mother, I did not know *shining* was so beautiful.

ASA. Son, you *see?*

JOAB (*bounding to his father and running fingers up and down him*). Father! (*He is like a fawn, glad and gay, as if only beauty and gladness existed.*)

ASA (*voice stern with awe*). How did you get your sight?

JOAB (*without stopping his darting from one object to another, and bending down to run his hand about the cheek of a little boy who clings to him*). I sat right where you put me, father, by my column in Solomon's porch. Oh! (*He draws the little boy to him and they hug in an ecstasy of joy.*) Oh, little John, how sweet you are! (*He keeps his arm about the boy and, as other children crowd about, he touches them affectionately as he talks.*) Some men were coming and I held out my bowl. I heard one of them ask who had sinned — you, father, or mother, or I, and, oh, I was so angry. They cannot say my mother sinned. Then, suddenly, another man spoke, and ah — (*his face is radiant*). *What* a voice! I can tell, by men's voices, whether they are good and friendly, or bad and dangerous. This man's voice — it was strong. I knew he must be big. It was an outdoor voice — like a man who had slept on the ground and climbed mountains. He was no weakling, like me, and yet his voice was full of friendship, as if he *liked* you, though he spoke quite sharp to the man who asked the question. Short and sharp he answered, as if he knew what he was talking about, and what do you suppose he said? *Nobody* had sinned, but that the work of God is going to be seen. I felt the strangest, most thrilling *something*, and then he was stooping over me and putting mud on my eyelids and he spoke — oh so kindly, and yet with command: " Go. Wash in Siloam."

JUDITH. Oh, my son, you *didn't?* Not alone?

JOAB. Mother, I *had* to. If you had heard his voice, you'd know I *had* to. (*He looks down at the eager child who snuggles close to him and he lifts a dark curl wonderingly, exchanging a loving smile with the boy.*)

JUDITH. But you *promised!* Oh, the danger!

ASA. Hush, Judith. And then?

(*From time to time, as he goes on with his story, one or another of the neighbors pushes up and touches him in friendly congratulation. He nods brightly and lovingly to each without interrupting his tale. All through this scene there is a happy exchange of glances and handclasps, showing him to be beloved by all. The little boy keeps his place close.*)

JOAB. He went off with his friends and I got up and tried to start. Oh, I was frightened. I had never found my way alone.

JUDITH (*looking at* ANNA). Never.

JOAB (*tweaking the boy's ear and laughing with him like a boy*). And I didn't want to disobey you, mother. It was dreadful, all alone, and I almost gave up, but *something* made me keep on. It was the ring in his voice I couldn't forget. I kept feeling my way and getting all turned about, and lost, and then I was at the steps and I knew I had found the pool. I threw off my cloak, mother, and plunged right in. (*All during this recital the little boy has watched his face with grave intensity. At the triumphant end of the tale, his little face lights up and he and* JOAB *exchange a happy hug.*)

JUDITH. Oh! Oh! In the water! All by yourself!

JOAB. It was terrible, the plunge, but I got my sight! Oh, mother! (*He picks up the little boy and swings him high above his head to the shrieking joy of the child. All the others are awed and solemn, but* JOAB *and the boy laugh and shout like young and happy gods in a crowd of terrified mortals.*)

(*Enter* HILKIAH *U.R.*)

ASA (*bowing to ground*).   Master!

JUDITH (*bending low*).   My lord!

ASA.   You honor my poor house.

HILKIAH (*looking rapidly about and pointing to* JOAB).   Is that your son, Asa?

ASA.   My only son, sir. (*Short and sharp to* JOAB) Son, this is my master.

JOAB (*pleasantly but without awe*).   Sir (*he nods brightly*).

HILKIAH.   Was he ever blind?

JUDITH.   Born blind, sir.

HILKIAH.   It *is* your son, the *same* son?

ASA.   Our only son, my lord.

HILKIAH (*to crowd*).   You, here, do you know this boy?

NEIGHBORS.   Yes.

FIRST NEIGHBOR (*stepping out*).   Yes, my lord, I know him.

HILKIAH (*sharply to another*).   You? Do you know him? (*The* SECOND NEIGHBOR, *who is an old bald man, shakes his head with deliberate obstinacy.*)   Well, did you know the son of these people?

SECOND NEIGHBOR.   Oh, yes, your honor, I knew him very well.

HILKIAH.   So? It isn't the same?

SECOND NEIGHBOR.   No, sir. This is a different boy. (*At this an excited pantomime of argument begins in crowd.*)

HILKIAH.   How different?

SECOND NEIGHBOR.   Well, for one thing, this fellow is a foot taller. (JOAB *and the boy punch each other and laugh.*)

JUDITH.   He does look taller, standing so straight. His blindness made him stoop.

SECOND NEIGHBOR.   Oh, it isn't only that. This boy's got spirit. Joab is a poor devil.

JOAB (*with a gay laugh*).   *Wasn't* I, Eliakim?

FIRST NEIGHBOR.   It's Joab, sir, I'd know him anywhere. We all know him.

JUDITH (*fiercely to* SECOND NEIGHBOR). I guess I know my own son. (*The quarrel becomes general in pantomime and* JOAB *and the little boy poke each other and enjoy the fun.*)

SECOND NEIGHBOR. Oh, I admit the fellow looks like Joab — *some.* Not much when you look at him close.

FIRST NEIGHBOR. 'Tis too Joab.

SECOND NEIGHBOR. 'Tain't, I tell you.

JOAB (*laughing and swinging boy about*). Oh, ho! Eliakim, you don't know me! That's rich!

HILKIAH. Are you or are you not Joab, the son of Asa?

JOAB (*instantly sober, standing straight, one arm about boy*). Sir, I am he.

HILKIAH. Were you blind?

JOAB. Oh, yes, sir — blind.

HILKIAH. Are you sure you see now?

JOAB. I see! I see!

HILKIAH (*looking close into his eyes*). Are you sure?

JOAB (*face radiant*). Sure.

HILKIAH. Well, if you really see, what do I look like?

JOAB (*gravely*). You, sir? It's rather hard for me to say. I haven't seen much in this world, yet. I kept my eyes almost closed till I got home because I wanted my mother's face to be the first. (*He looks lovingly at* JUDITH.) But there was one thing I did see, coming, and I *think*, sir, you're like that.

HILKIAH (*kindly*). Indeed, what was it?

JOAB. It was a palm tree. I know, because I have passed it many times, felt it, and asked my mother what it was. She told me it was a palm tree.

HILKIAH (*pleased*). Well, so I remind you of a palm tree? A royal palm. In what way?

JOAB (*without thought of impudence*). Well, sir, the trunk's hard, like stone. It looks dead all the way up, but when you get to the top (*he shakes his finger craftily*) — look out! It's alive *there*. It isn't thrilling with life, the way you expect a tree to be — not full of warm, friendly life, like common trees — like all these friends of ours here (*he smiles very sweetly at neighbors*) — but, all the same, there's life at the top (*he taps head significantly*) — for all it looks so dead. (*He beams at* HILKIAH, *hoping he is pleased.*)

HILKIAH. Well! Really!

ASA (*in frightened reproval*). Why, Joab! (*This is a great moment for the crowd, hearing someone who dares speak up to an aristocrat. They are scared but delighted, and* ANNA *cannot repress a quick giggle, though she instantly claps hand over mouth.* JOAB *and the children are the only ones who do not sense a tense situation.*)

JOAB (*pleasantly*). Have I said anything amiss? He *asked*, and it's all I have seen that seems like him. (*He looks about.*) Now, this bench, he's not like that, father. That's lowly and serving, like you, father. (*He takes up bowl.*) Or this bowl! (*He holds it high in two hands.*) You'd never say he was like *this!* Now, would you? *Shining!* This is like — (*face radiant*). You know, I didn't *see* the man who cured me, father. He was gone when I came seeing, but I heard his voice and I *think* he must look like this. (*He gazes in admiration at bowl.*) *Shining!*

HILKIAH (*too fine to be much offended*). Then you didn't see the man?

JOAB. No, sir.

HILKIAH. Well, I *did*, and I want to warn you, boy, that he's a dangerous fellow. Asa, I am afraid this is going to get you into trouble. I mean to help you if I can.

JOAB. Where did he go?

HILKIAH (*for the first time showing bitterness*). He went into the temple, after breaking the Sabbath — the blasphemer!

JOAB. How did he break the Sabbath?

HILKIAH. Why, by curing you, boy. That was work, wasn't it?

JOAB. Oh, that was the work of God. He said so. I know

it was, anyway, because I felt it *here*, inside me. Nobody but God could get *inside* you, could they?

HILKIAH (*with restrained patience.*) He put mud on your eyes. That was working.

JOAB (*trustfully*). But it wasn't the mud cured. It was what happened *inside*. The mud on my eyelids made me know something was going to happen, and then it did; but it was God worked.

HILKIAH. Hush, my boy. God doesn't work.

JOAB. *He* said he did.

JUDITH. Oh, my darling, you mustn't —

HILKIAH (*stern for the first time*). You, born in sin, are you trying to teach *me?*

JOAB. In the temple, you said? I'll find him. He'll know. (*He drops the boy's hand and runs off U.R. gaily, the crowd making way for him.* JUDITH *starts after him, but* ASA *pulls her back.*)

JUDITH (*pulling away*). Oh, if anything should happen!

ASA. He isn't blind, *now*.

HILKIAH. Let him go. Clear out these people. (*He makes authoritative gesture to crowd, which moves out U.R., with curious backward looks. The little boy with his mother is the last to leave.*)

HILKIAH. Asa, this is a serious matter. When the thing happened and I was told it was your boy, I came to warn you. (*The parents bow low.*) We had a meeting of the leading citizens last night. You know. You brought in the wine. It took a mighty lot to warm them up. (*He smiles genially.*)

ASA (*gravely*). Yes, my lord, and it was your best — the oldest. I wondered, sir, if you meant so much.

HILKIAH. Well, to tell the truth, I didn't. I hadn't any idea it would take so long to come to a decision. There was more opposition — but we finally settled it to recommend to the Sanhedrin that anyone who acknowledges this carpenter shall be excommunicated.

JUDITH (*with scorn*). Oh, the disgrace!

HILKIAH (*with a meaning look*). Yes, my girl, disgrace and worse.

JUDITH (*realizing that she is involved and terror-stricken*). Oh, sir, we've always been respectable. I couldn't bear disgrace.

HILKIAH (*kindly*). No, and I don't want you to. That's why I came. Asa is valuable to me. No man ever had a more faithful servant. (*The men exchange a look of confidence as* ASA *bows low.*) I couldn't let harm come to his home.

ASA. I thank you, my lord, most humbly. (*He kisses border of robe.*)

JUDITH (*greatly excited*). Why, sir, if you're cast out of the synagogue, there can't anybody give you fire or water. Nobody can *speak* to you, and, at the well, my lord, where I go for my water, who'd help me get my jar back onto my head after it's full? Women *have* to help each other with the lifting, your honor. You can *carry* a full jar, once it's on your head, but you can't put it on your head alone. (*She illustrates with many gestures.*)

HILKIAH. Now, don't be frightened. I can get you out of it, if you'll do exactly as I say.

JUDITH (*kissing his robe*). It's most noble of you, sir.

HILKIAH. Did you see this man?

ASA. No, master.

JUDITH (*with frightened vehemence*). No, *never.*

HILKIAH. Never spoke with him? (*They shake their heads in energetic and frightened denial.*) You don't know anything about his healing your son?

JUDITH. No, sir, only our boy *said* —

HILKIAH. Never mind what he said. Be careful to tell only what you *know.* Nothing else.

ASA. We don't know one thing except he is our son and was born blind and now he can see.

HILKIAH (*relieved*). Oh, well, then, stick to that when you're brought before the council.

JUDITH (*with shriek*). Before the council? Oh, sir, they won't make us go, will they? We haven't done any harm. We're very particular. We keep Sabbath and we tithe, *always*. I *never* miss — (*Her conscience accuses.*) Well — once I did, but — now, there's a *neighbor* of ours and *she* —

ASA (*sharp*). Hush!

JUDITH (*angry and frightened*). You don't think I was going to *tell* on her, do you? Only, if there's folks got to go before the Sanhedrin —

HILKIAH. You'll have to go.

JUDITH (*whimpering like a child fearing a beating*). What'll they *do* to us?

HILKIAH. Nothing, if you stick to it that you don't know this man and don't know how your boy got over his blindness.

ASA. But we do, master. He told us.

HILKIAH. No, Asa. You don't know anything except what you have seen for yourself. Be blind to everything else and you'll be safe.

ASA (*looking front and speaking in a whisper as if he sensed a deeper meaning*). Blind and safe?

JUDITH. But my boy? Will he have to go before the council?

HILKIAH. Yes.

JUDITH. Oh, sir, they won't cast him out! He couldn't help it!

HILKIAH. Not if he'll say what I tell him to say.

JUDITH (*eagerly*). He will! He will!

ASA. Doesn't the Sanhedrin want the truth, sir?

HILKIAH. We know the truth, Asa. We've made a thorough investigation.

ASA. But a man who can heal the blind, my lord?

HILKIAH. Give God the glory. As for this fellow, he is a sinner and a danger to our nation. I know, Asa. I, myself, have given valuable time to listen to his talk so that we should be certain of our facts, though we have had spies, for a long time, bringing us every word. I have heard the fellow utter blasphemies about Jehovah that made my blood run cold. With my own ears I heard him tell a shocking story to show what Jehovah was like. It was about a man who had two sons — one decent and one bad. The bad one went off and lived a loose, wicked life till he'd spent all his money and, finally, got work *feeding pigs.*

JUDITH (*nose elevated in disgust*). Ohhh!

HILKIAH. Yes! A *Jew* taking care of pigs! Can you get anything lower than that? Well, he finally started for home, meaning to own up how bad he'd been and take his punishment, but, if you'll believe it, his father was watching for him (JUDITH *is so entranced with the story that she has entirely forgotten everything else and shows by her wide eyes and ecstatic expression how delighted and absorbed she is*) and ran out to meet him. (JUDITH *claps her hands.*) And never gave the fellow a chance to say he was sorry for his disgusting conduct, but he ordered the servants to dress him up in the best clothes they had, and jewelry, and invited a big company to meet him. (JUDITH *likes it better and better.*) And when the older brother — the decent one — very properly objected, the father said: "This my son was lost and is found. Of course we must be glad."

JUDITH (*clapping hands*). Oh, what a lovely story!

HILKIAH. But he was talking about *God.*

JUDITH (*face falling*). Oh, well, of course —

HILKIAH. If men are to do as they please and then have a fuss made over them —

JUDITH (*wistfully*). I suppose God is very angry with us, sir, when we sin?

HILKIAH. Of course, and nothing but the fear of God's wrath will make people behave.

JUDITH. Yes, I know I wouldn't tithe every little thing if I wasn't afraid. Would you, sir? (*She is curious to know whether he really does.*)

HILKIAH. No, that's it. This young man is spreading dangerous ideas, and the worst of it is that our boys are listening to him. It's got to stop and it's going to stop.

ASA. It was good of him to cure my son, but I wish he hadn't done it on the Sabbath.

HILKIAH. Oh, well, he says the Sabbath isn't of any consequence.

JUDITH (*with a shocked squeal as she claps hand over mouth*). Ohhh! (*She is, however, more curious than shocked.*) Tell me some more he said, sir.

(*Enter* JOAB *U.R., with the crowd behind him and the little boy beside him, his arm about the child. He is full of joy and confidence.*)

JOAB. It *was* God that worked. I *knew* that was what he said. I found him, sir. He heard that I was going to be cast out of the synagogue and he was looking for me. Wasn't that kind of him? Oh, mother, you *must* see him. His face *is* shining like a bowl — only different.

HILKIAH. So he's heard about the excommunication, has he?

JOAB (*cheerfully*). Yes, but I told him he needn't worry about *that*. They'd never cast anybody out because he wasn't blind any more, would they, sir? (*He laughs at the absurdity of the idea, but* ANNA *grasps Judith's hand and they exchange a quick, anxious glance.*) God working in us — wanting to make us beautiful! Isn't that thrilling, mother? Oh, I knelt at his feet and begged him to let me stay with him always, like the young men who were with him when he cured me.

HILKIAH. So you are his disciple, are you? (JOAB *shakes his head with a sober face.*) Why not?

JOAB. He wouldn't let me. He said I had leaned on other people too long as it was. If I stayed with him the spirit of God wouldn't have a chance to grow in me.

HILKIAH. God — a chance! Fire of Gehenna, what do you mean?

JOAB. Why, you see the kingdom of heaven isn't a *place*, way off *here* (*he flings out his right arm*) — or *there* (*he flings out his left*). He says it is inside us and it has to have a chance to grow. He said it was something like yeast that my mother puts into leavened bread. At first, it doesn't seem it's going to do a thing, but, in the end, it raises the whole lump.

HILKIAH. Well, of all the disgusting talk! It's worse than I feared.

JOAB. Of course it's a new idea. I always thought God was way off somewhere, sitting on a gold throne and watching us close to see that we didn't skip any of the rules. It's so different I was afraid I didn't understand enough to go on without him, but he said, yes, I did. All you need is to *begin* giving God a chance.

HILKIAH. God — a chance! Sacrilege!

JOAB. No, it's true, I know. It was my faith gave God a chance to cure my blindness. He said so. I felt it. It was like a well of healing springing up inside me. God working.

HILKIAH. Stop, boy! God doesn't work. Servants work, and slaves and poor people. Jehovah is a mighty Ruler lifted up above the circle of the heavens.

JOAB. That's what I used to think, too, sir, but it's wrong. He knows — he said he did. I can tell you it's good news for us poor people that God loves us and is as interested in us as he is in rich people and nobility.

HILKIAH. The man must be mad.

ANNA. Could a madman open the eyes of the blind?

ASA. Perhaps he has to be a little mad to do it.

JOAB. He isn't mad. He's just as quiet and *plain*. He says —

HILKIAH. I don't want to hear any more what he says. I want to know what you are going to say, young man, when you're brought before the Sanhedrin.

JOAB (*delighted*). Oh, shall I be taken to the Sanhedrin?

HILKIAH. Yes.

JOAB. Father! Think of that! (*He looks about at his friends in ingenuous pleasure.*) The council wants to hear about my cure. Oh, sir, I'm glad, though my cure isn't really the important thing. What matters is God — his being friendly and near —

HILKIAH. Enough!

JOAB. Very well, sir, I'll save the rest for the Sanhedrin. I hope I can tell it right, but it's so big and so different —

HILKIAH. You've just one thing to tell the council and that is that you don't know one thing about the man who cured you. You don't know who he is nor where he came from, do you?

JOAB. Why, no, sir. I didn't think to ask.

HILKIAH. Say so, then.

JOAB. But that isn't the important thing — who he is. What matters is that he was sent by God. He told me so. And you see, sir, if a man's sent by God, it's the message that counts — the good news —

HILKIAH. Young man, I'll have you understand the Sanhedrin isn't interested in news.

JOAB. Aren't they? Well, after all, they're not so important. This good news changes everything, because if God is *in* everybody, why, a man's likely to pop up anywhere with God working in him like yeast. It's a big idea, isn't it, father?

ASA. Too big, my son.

JOAB. How could it be too big?

ASA. Too much life in it.

JOAB. Life! Yes, he spoke about life — abundant life. He said he had come that we should have abundant life. Doesn't the Sanhedrin want abundant life, sir? (HILKIAH *throws up his hands in despair of the boy's ignorance. He looks, not unkindly, at* ASA.)

ASA (*gently*). My son, your blindness has kept you from understanding the real world you live in.

JUDITH. I didn't want you to know, my darling. (JOAB *looks from one to the other in astonishment. The neighbors nod their heads wisely.*)

ASA. We thought to spare you suffering. You had enough

with your blindness. (*He looks sadly into his eyes, hands on shoulders.*) But now that you see, Joab —

JOAB (*frightened by their seriousness*). Father, what do you mean?

ASA. There's things in this world that have to be preserved — preserved at all cost — old things. Abundant life you talk about would sweep them away.

JOAB. How would it?

ASA. How can I explain? (*Thinks.*) Remember helping your mother sew new skins for the wine every fall?

JOAB (*return of old gaiety*). Yes, mother said I made good ones, too. I *liked* helping.

ASA. Why did we have to make new ones each time?

JOAB. Oh, the new wine, when it got working, would burst the old, dried — (*Something in his father's face arrests him, and slowly the truth dawns.*) You mean abundant life would burst — ?

ASA (*hand on Joab's arm*). My son, sight has come to you. It is a blessing, but don't see too much.

JOAB (*looking front, his eyes wide with a new fear*). All my life afraid of darkness, must I now fear the light?

ASA. There's more danger in it. (*Father and son stand facing each other with tragic understanding, but* JUDITH *does not understand and is impatient.*)

JUDITH. Asa, what are you talking about? There isn't one bit of danger if Joab says exactly what your kind master tells him to. Prince Hilkiah is a very wise man. You couldn't have a better adviser.

JOAB. But I have.

JUDITH. Who?

JOAB. My father.

JUDITH. Oh, well, your father wants you to do as the prince says.

JOAB. I mean God.

JUDITH (*shocked*).   I don't like to hear you speak that way about God.

JOAB.   But that's the whole point of the good news, mother. All my life I have been led by others, but now I know I have a Guide within.   I see.

ASA.   Don't try to see too far, at first, boy. (*He takes his hand.*)

HILKIAH.   You have one duty, and only one — to obey your parents. So long as a man lives, he is subject to his parents. It is the law.

JOAB.   The law of Moses, but there is a higher law.

HILKIAH.   What?

JOAB.   The law of a man's own soul — the Father within —

JUDITH.   How could a law be higher than Moses?

JOAB.   A greater than Moses has spoken to me, mother. I have had an experience of the truth that God works in me. He charged me that I must be true to the light — even — why, he said if a man lived the way he did, he'd have to be willing to hate his father and mother —

HILKIAH.   Horrible!

JUDITH (*wailing*).   After all I've sacrificed for you.

JOAB (*gently*).   Try to understand, mother dear. He didn't mean it that way. It was only that he knew how dependent I had been and now — why, there is a higher law than the law of obedience to parents — the law of a man's own soul.

HILKIAH.   Young man, when you are cast out of the synagogue, no one will give you so much as a drink of water, or a coal to light your fire. (JOAB *does not understand. He looks puzzled.* HILKIAH *beckons to crowd to come down.*)

ASA.   For a little time yet, my son, you must lean upon others. You have never worked. You have no trade. Among strangers you would starve. Your own people will stand by you and help you to learn how, but the Romans are cruel. You would stand no chance with them.

JOAB.   Cast out? Out of my own *people?* Out of my own *home?* That is impossible. I do not believe it. (*He turns to neighbors*) Why, you are all my old friends. You would not go back on me? (*The crowd stands sullen without reply.*)

HILKIAH.   Every Jewish door will be shut against you and you will be driven from the temple porch where you have so long sat with your begging bowl.

JUDITH.   The disgrace! No decent life after once having been outcast. I could not bear it.

ASA.   Dear boy, I understand the struggle in your heart, but this world is too hard a place for perfect loyalty.

JUDITH (*pleading*).   You wouldn't disgrace me, Joab?

JOAB.   What are you asking of me, oh, my mother?

HILKIAH (*sternly*).   Silence, nothing more. When they question you, you do not know.

JOAB (*half to himself*).   One thing I know: I was blind, now I see.

HILKIAH (*eagerly*).   Say that, but as for this Jesus — silence.

ASA.   You do not need to lie. In gratitude for all the weary years our hands have led you, be silent for our sakes. *Afterward*, follow the voice, but now —

JOAB (*his arm still about the little boy, who looks up in wonder at the seriousness of his face*).   When the call comes, if you do not answer it who knows whether it will come again? Who was it that said: " Seek the Lord while he may be found. Call upon him while he is near "?

HILKIAH.   The prophet Isaiah.

JOAB.   He knew.

ASA.   They killed him for knowing — cut him in four pieces.

JOAB.   Oh —

ASA (*desperately*).   If you want to be safe in this world, don't see too much, and what you do see, don't talk about.

HILKIAH (*sternly*).   You must decide. Stand by this stranger and every friend you have in the world will desert you. Here, you! (*to the neighbors*). If this young man is cast out, how will you treat him? (*The crowd gives a low growl and draws back as one man.*) You will not speak to him?

CROWD. No.

HILKIAH. You will not feed him?

CROWD (*with stronger voice*). No.

HILKIAH. You will not warm him by your fire nor give him a drink from the well?

CROWD (*in a fanatic shout*). No, no!

HILKIAH. Henceforth he is accurst, a vagrant, and an exile from home and country, and if one of you so much as speaks a word of pity in his ear, that one, too, is outcast. (*The mother of the little boy grabs him hastily by the arm and drags him away. The child tries to cling to* JOAB, *but cannot.* JOAB *looks at them all in amazement.*)

JOAB. Why, Anna? Mary? Eliakim? Little John? (*To each he reaches out arms of pleading and is repulsed by each.*) You would not go back on me, my old friends? You have always been so kind to me, helping me in my blindness. (*His voice becomes desperate in pleading*) How could I do without your friendship?

HILKIAH. They must desert you. They have no other choice if they would live. Speak, men.

CROWD (*pushing back*). Ugh! Outcast!

JOAB (*reaches out his arms to the little boy, but the child has become frightened by the abhorrence of the crowd and shrinks away from him, clinging to his mother's skirts and hiding his head*). My little John, too? Father? Mother? (*He turns to his parents in agony of pleading*) You will stand by? You would not have me disown the man who gave sight to my eyes and to my soul?

HILKIAH (*not without sympathy*). Father and mother must disown you. They dare not otherwise.

JOAB (*holding out his arms in frightened and heartbroken pleading*). Father! (ASA *shakes his head slowly and sadly, but he draws back.*) Mother? (*it is the cry of a terrified child. He is about to fling himself upon her breast, but she, too, draws back.* JOAB *is horrified.*)

HILKIAH.   Is a stranger worth giving up all this for?

JOAB (*slowly*).   Yes, he is worth it.

HILKIAH.   Very well.   You must choose.

ASA (*stretching out his arms*).   Joab!   Just this once shut your eyes for my sake.

JUDITH (*with a broken cry of pleading*).   *Son!*

JOAB.   Oh, warm and friendly blindness, is *this* the price of seeing?

HILKIAH (*sternly but still not unkindly*).   It is the price.

JOAB (*eyes turned slowly front and kept at gallery level*). Then I will pay it, but oh, God in heaven, I did not know that seeing cost so high a price.

CURTAIN

THE GREAT CHOICE*

An Incident of the Next War

by

Fred Eastman

FOREWORD

" Those who would take their bearings in this modern world, sooner or later must see how devotion to the state is related to the devotion which is due the eternal God. How far is it possible to give to Caesar that which belongs to God alone? " So writes Edward Shillito.

One may devoutly hope that his nation and his religion may never be in opposition. But, as Jaggers says in Dickens' *Great Expectations*, " devoutly hoping is pious but not to the point." The two devotions do come into conflict. Such a conflict makes the central struggle of this play. It is a conflict which grows more vital and insistent with every passing year. On the one side is nationalism with its creed of " My country, right or wrong." On the other side is religion with its first commandment, " Thou shalt have no other gods before me." Between the two ultimately lies a great choice.

The ancient Greeks knew this conflict and Sophocles in the fifth century B.C. built his play *Antigone* around it. The present play is modeled after *Antigone*. A part of the dialogue is a free adaptation of Sophocles' lines, but it lacks entirely the epic surge of his verse. Whatever strength it has may be credited to Sophocles. Its weaknesses are original. If one should ask, Why model a play about the next war after one written twenty-four hundred years ago? the answer is that the theme, the situation and the central struggle are the same. It seems fitting therefore to use the structure which Sophocles used so effectively in presenting these. However, changes in custom have necessitated certain changes in plot and treatment. And new characters, even when dominated by old ideas, have a way of taking control of a play and determining its outcome quite irrespective of ancient models or of modern author.

F. E.

CHARACTERS

PAULA
ANNE GOODMAN
ISABEL GOODMAN
THOMAS KRUGER
MISS LEE
A LIEUTENANT
HERMAN KRUGER
REV. ROBERT THOMPSON

Scene: The private office of Thomas Kruger, civilian commander of the Middle West Region. (The play assumes that in the next war the entire country will be mobilized and, for purposes of administration, divided into regions, each under a civilian commander with well-nigh dictatorial powers.)

Time: During the next war.

THE GREAT CHOICE

The curtain rises upon the private office of Thomas Kruger. It is an office of simple dignity. The furniture, all of walnut, consists of Kruger's flat-top desk on the right, a small table on the left laden with magazines and newspapers neatly arranged, and three chairs for visitors. Also a map-globe upon a stand of its own. Across the left wall is draped an American flag. A door in this wall near the rear leads to the outer office. A window in the center of the rear wall looks out upon the avenue. The rest of the wall space is lined with bookshelves reaching to the ceiling — every foot of them filled with books. Most of them are books on economics, politics, sociology and allied subjects, with here and there a sprinkling of volumes on international law. The top of Kruger's desk is clear except for a telephone, an appointment calendar, a tooled leather desk set, and a leather-covered flat file or work-organizer for current papers.

The door opens and PAULA *ushers in* ANNE *and* ISABEL. PAULA *is a model secretary of about twenty-five. Her glance is quick and alert, and the impression she makes is of a girl whose ambition is to anticipate her employer's needs.* ANNE, *a girl of twenty-three, good-looking but not pretty, thoroughly alive and determined, is dressed in a simple and rather mannish suit, but it is apparent that dress is not a major interest with her. She is above medium height and of athletic carriage, and the erectness of her head makes her seem taller than she is. No one needs look at the two girls more than once to see that* ANNE *is the leader who knows what she wants and expects to get it, while* ISABEL *is the follower. Yet* ISABEL *might be easier to live with, for she is quiet and affectionate. Two years younger than* ANNE, *she has probably been dominated by her in home and school. She is an inch or*

two shorter than ANNE *and her hair is darker.   Just now she
seems puzzled as to what* ANNE *may be about to do.*

PAULA (*showing them in*).   In here, please.   Young Mr.
Kruger will be back shortly, and I will bring him to you.   (ISABEL
sits L.C.   ANNE *remains standing, in front of Kruger's desk.*)

ANNE.   Thanks, Paula, but it isn't the young Mr. Kruger
we want — right now, at least.   It's his father.

PAULA.   Ah, his father?   About — about — ?

ANNE.   About our brother, John.   He's been arrested, you
know.

PAULA.   I know.   Is there anything I can do?   Anything
that would save Mr. Kruger's time?

ANNE.   The morning papers say that Mr. Kruger expects
to make an example of John.   Do you think that is true, Paula?

PAULA.   That is the statement he made to the press.

ISABEL (*anxiously*).   Just what will they do to John?

PAULA.   I can't say.   But I know that Mr. Kruger feels that
he must put a stop to his activities.   He is obstructing the war.

ANNE.   I know Mr. Kruger's point of view.   What I want,
Paula, is a chance to see John and talk with him.   We tried at
the guardhouse over there at the camp (*indicating a camp
visible from the window*) but were told that we would have to
have a special permit.   I didn't know where to go, but Mr.
Kruger's position as civilian commander for this region makes
him just about all-powerful, and I thought he would be willing
to arrange a pass for me to see John.

PAULA.   I see.   Do you think you can persuade John to
change his — ah — his attitude?

ANNE.   I'm afraid not, Paula.   But I am his sister, and
surely I have a right to see him when he's in trouble?

PAULA.   Mr. Kruger wouldn't object if I gave you a note to
headquarters, and it would save his time.   If you will wait here,
I will write it and bring it to you.

ANNE.   Thank you, Paula.   You are very helpful.

PAULA. I should like to be. (*Exits L.*)

ISABEL (*anxiously*). What are you up to, Anne?

ANNE. A matter of life and death.

ISABEL. Oh, surely not! The worst they can do to John is to put him in prison, and after all maybe he would be safer there —

ANNE. I mean life and death — not prison. If Kruger finds out that John is really the head of this international movement of youth to stop the war, he will have him shot. Herman told me last night that his father knows that the youth movement has its headquarters in this city, and the government wants him to break it up and make an example of the leaders.

ISABEL. But they don't kill people for belonging to a youth movement, even if it is pacifist. Not in America.

ANNE. They didn't in the last war. But the government after three years of this war has grown desperate. The new ruling for men of military age is fight or die.

ISABEL. Oh, dear, what can we do?

ANNE. We must help John to escape.

ISABEL (*shocked*). Escape? But how?

ANNE. There is no time to lose. Here is my plan. (*She draws nearer and speaks cautiously*) If I can manage to see John in his cell, I will make him exchange clothes with me. I'll take a mourning veil to hide his face. I'll have a taxi at the curb. You wait in the taxi and give the orders to the driver, so he won't suspect anything from hearing John's voice. Then drive to Field's store. I'll arrange for one of the other leaders to pick him up there.

ISABEL (*in distress*). Oh, Anne! Anne! You can't do that sort of thing these days. You'll be caught and get in trouble yourself.

ANNE (*sharply*). Do you have any better plan?

ISABEL. No, but —

ANNE. Then let's follow this one. An hour from now may be too late.

ISABEL (*more distressed*). Listen, Anne. I'd do anything

for John. I love him as much as you do. But I can't see this. It's rash.

ANNE (*rather scornfully*). Rash or not, I'm going to do it. I'm no coward.

ISABEL. Our family has sacrificed enough. When the Chinese killed father and mother I knew it was the price missionaries sometimes have to pay for their religion. When Robert was killed in action I accepted it as the price of patriotism. But now John is in the guardhouse, and you propose to risk —

ANNE (*unrelenting*). I'll not urge you. Make your choice.

ISABEL (*near to tears*). I can't, I can't.

ANNE. I'll go it alone, then. I can arrange the little matter of the taxi without your help.

ISABEL (*pleading*). Oh, Anne, don't, don't! If they would take his life for obstructing the war, won't they do the same to you?

ANNE. Very likely. But we come of a stock that is not afraid to face death. I don't propose to let them kill my brother if I can help it.

ISABEL. Of course not. But can't you trust God to help John and do what is best for us all?

ANNE (*impatiently*). No. It's because the good people of the country have been content to trust and then *do* nothing that we are in this mess. If we had used the brains He gave us and shown a little of His energy and courage, we wouldn't have had another world war.

ISABEL. I can't argue, Anne. But I'm afraid for you — afraid.

ANNE. You needn't be. Fear for yourself. I can take care of myself.

ISABEL. If you fail?

ANNE. I'll take the consequences.

ISABEL. Is it wise to attempt the impossible?

ANNE. How do I know it's impossible until I try?

ISABEL. I don't mean that. You might get him out this time.

But you are setting yourself — one lone girl — against the whole country. Do you think that's possible?

ANNE. Well, I'm doing it.

ISABEL (*resigning the struggle and wiping the tears from her eyes*). Oh, Anne. You're a fool — but John will love you for it, and I don't blame him.

ANNE (*quickly*). Hush — (*Re-enter* PAULA *with a note, which she hands to* ANNE.)

PAULA. If you will take this to the regimental headquarters tent — that's the large one with the flag over it, just across the street at the entrance to the park (*she points to it*) — I think they will issue a pass at once for you to see your brother.

ANNE. That's very kind of you, Paula. Thank you. Good day. (*She goes out L., determination in her step.* ISABEL *follows doubtfully. The telephone rings.* PAULA *answers.*)

PAULA (*at the desk phone*). Mr. Kruger's secretary speaking. — Yes, Doctor Thompson, what can I do for you? — I think so. He's not in now, but he will be here shortly. Would two-thirty be convenient? — Very well. I'll put it upon his calendar. He's always glad to see you —

(*Enter* KRUGER *L., a tall man, grizzled gray, about fifty-eight or sixty years of age. He strides to his seat at the desk.*)

KRUGER. Herman come in yet?

PAULA. Not yet.

KRUGER. See that article of his in last night's *World?*

PAULA. Yes, it was splendid, wasn't it?

KRUGER. Clear-cut, objective, detached, not a word wasted. The boy is a real journalist.

PAULA. You are proud of him, aren't you? Mr. Bellamy says he's a chip off the old block.

KRUGER. He's a block off the old chip. Some day — but let's get to work.

PAULA. Very well. I've put the clippings from the morning papers in your file there. Both chains of newspapers carried in full your story about John Goodman.

KRUGER. Good. The country's aroused about these obstructors. It's time to handle them without gloves.

PAULA (*at the door and glancing into the outer office*). I think the young woman you spoke of is already here.

KRUGER. Show her in. (*While* PAULA *is bringing* MISS LEE, KRUGER *glances hastily through the clippings and nods his satisfaction.* MISS LEE *is a young woman of twenty-eight, goodlooking and alert.*)

PAULA. Miss Lee.

KRUGER (*rising*). How do you do, Miss Lee? Did you bring back the bacon?

MISS LEE. Here it is. Documentary evidence. (*She takes from her brief case a sheaf of papers and pamphlets.*)

KRUGER. I'll look at that later. Give me the substance of it orally.

MISS LEE. We have had three under-cover operatives working on this international youth movement for six months, and I think there is enough evidence here to blow it sky-high.

KRUGER. On what ground?

MISS LEE. Deliberate intention to obstruct the war.

KRUGER. Not simply Christian scruples about bearing arms?

MISS LEE. No. They go much further. And they aren't confined to Christians at all. Jews, Mohammedans, Buddhists, Confucianists — they are all in it together. They not only won't fight — they are trying to persuade others not to fight.

KRUGER. Do they use violent methods?

MISS LEE. Non-violent. Gandhi stuff.

KRUGER. The hardest kind to deal with.

MISS LEE. But the most insidious.

KRUGER. Anything new in their line of talk?

MISS LEE. The same old thing — that wars are stirred up to defend economic policies that are indefensible. The mistakes of capitalism. The alleged fallacies of nationalism.

KRUGER. Communistic?

MISS LEE. Some are. Others fairly conservative.

KRUGER. Who are the leaders?

MISS LEE. They are well organized — a chapter in nearly every city throughout the world. But the leader of the whole outfit is right here in your own town. If you can cut him off, you will cut the head off the whole organization.

KRUGER. His name?

MISS LEE. Goodman — John Goodman.

KRUGER (*triumphantly*). I've got him! Nabbed him last night. I've been suspecting all this and that boy in particular, but I didn't have proof. You have it there? Sure?

MISS LEE. No doubt about it. Here's the manuscript of a pamphlet he circulates. It's in his own hand. We got it from the printers. Don't ask me how. They are still looking for it. And here's his history. He's been an internationalist ever since he was knee-high.

KRUGER (*looking over the manuscript hastily*). Why, some of this is straight treason! I know his history. Born in China. American missionaries for parents. Grew up with Chinese boys. His parents put his older brother in school in this country, and he turned out very well. Was killed in action last month. But they put this kid in school in China, and he turned out a Chinese practically. Thinks more of his yellow playmates than of Americans.

MISS LEE. It will be quite a feather in your cap to have caught him. Now that you've got him you know what to do with him. You have a reputation for speed in such matters.

KRUGER. I know what the government wants, and it's right. But it isn't easy.

MISS LEE. Why not?

KRUGER. It isn't easy to take a young man's life. I have no stomach for it. The only way I can justify it is that the welfare of the country as a whole will benefit by the sacrifice of a few leaders of this opposition.

MISS LEE.　Good riddance, I'd say.

KRUGER.　Then, too, I like the boy, even though he's a dangerous fool.

MISS LEE.　Know him personally?

KRUGER.　Yes.　His sister is engaged to my son.

MISS LEE (*whistling softly*).　I see!　Hard luck!　Still — it's your job.

KRUGER.　I know — it's my job.　I'll have to see it through.

MISS LEE.　The army will do the actual executing.　That needn't bother.

KRUGER.　But I will have to face Anne Goodman. (*Re-enter* PAULA *in great excitement.*)

PAULA.　Mr. Kruger!　Mr. Kruger!

KRUGER.　Well, well, what is it?

PAULA.　John Goodman has escaped!　In his sister's clothes. They've brought her here in his.

KRUGER.　How did this happen?　Bring her in at once. (PAULA *beckons, and* ANNE, *dressed in her brother's clothes — dark suit, white negligee shirt, no collar — is brought in by a* LIEUTENANT. *She is handcuffed.*)

PAULA.　She and her sister were here this morning.　They wanted a pass in order to see John.　I thought to save your time and gave them a note to headquarters.

KRUGER (*angrily*).　You had no right to do anything of the sort.

ANNE (*interrupting*).　It is not Paula's fault, Mr. Kruger. She is in no way responsible.

KRUGER (*ignoring* ANNE).　Lieutenant, will you tell me just what happened?　Paula, take this down. (PAULA *takes down in shorthand all the following episode.*)

LIEUTENANT.　I was in charge of the prison guard.　This girl appears about a quarter of an hour ago with a pass to see young Goodman.　She had a veil over her face.　I gave her the once-over to see if she had a gun or anything, but she didn't. So I tells one of the guard to take her to Goodman.　A few minutes later back she comes — apparently — her veil still over her face. I saw her get in a taxi and drive off. A minute or two later that guard comes to me and says, "I think that girl put one over on us." So I goes and finds this girl in the prisoner's clothes, and the prisoner escaped.

KRUGER. Have you notified your officers and headquarters?

LIEUTENANT. I did, sir. First thing. Then the colonel told me to bring this girl straight to you for questioning, since it was through your office her pass came.

KRUGER. Anne, is this true?

ANNE (*her head high*). Quite true.

KRUGER. Is it a college prank you think you played?

ANNE. It was no prank.

KRUGER. Did you know that John was being held on a serious charge?

ANNE. What charge?

KRUGER. Treason.

ANNE. John was no traitor.

KRUGER. That was for his judges to decide. You knew that I had announced that he would be tried at once?

ANNE. It was in all the papers.

KRUGER. So you deliberately helped a man to escape who was being held on a charge of treason to his country?

ANNE. I helped free my brother to serve humanity.

KRUGER (*sternly*). This country is at war. The government has made me responsible for an important civilian part in the conduct of that war. Your brother and his organization have been enemies within our own borders, obstructing, thwarting, confusing the issues. So I ordered John's arrest and trial. I want to be quite sure that you knew all that.

ANNE. I knew it. But I am not so sure that your orders to carry on this war came from heaven.

KRUGER. My orders come from my country.

ANNE. And you obey your country, right or wrong?

KRUGER. My country, right or wrong!

ANNE.   Well, I don't. I love my country. But I love justice more, and freedom, and the cause of youth. You want to know if I knew the consequences of helping my brother escape — is that it?

KRUGER.   That's it.

ANNE.   I knew that I should be put to death. What of it? I would rather die than live on in the sort of world you and your kind are making.

KRUGER.   You are crazy!

ANNE.   Future generations — if there are any — may decide that you are the insane one.

KRUGER.   How do you make that out?

ANNE.   Because you set your country above every other —

KRUGER.   I do!

ANNE.   And men like you in every other country do the same with theirs. Each country goes out to get what it wants in the rest of the world. Your interests conflict; you go to war; you call upon the youth of your countries to fight your battles for you and give up their blood. That's where the insanity lies.

KRUGER.   The excuse of a lot of youngsters who are afraid to fight!

ANNE.   Afraid? Do you think my brother has less courage than you? You will hunt him down in time and kill him as a pack of wolves kills a wild deer. But until you bring him down I know what he will be doing.

KRUGER.   Get this, Paula.

PAULA.   I'm getting it all, sir.

ANNE.   Yes, and remember it too. My brother will be serving a higher law than the law of his country. He will be serving the God who is above all countries. He will be binding the youth of the world together in a fellowship of good-will. He will lead them to pledge not to fight each other. And I have helped him. This little bit. I'm proud that I did not fail.

KRUGER (*controlling his anger with difficulty*). It sounds very romantic, but it won't do. We are dealing with facts now.

We are facing enemies with bullets in their guns — not schoolgirl oratory. You have already said enough and done enough to be court-martialed. But I want to be merciful — for personal reasons which you will understand. I will give you one chance for your life.

ANNE. What chance? I have asked for none.

KRUGER. Throw yourself upon the mercy of the government for the crime you have committed in aiding your brother's escape. I'll make it as easy as I can for you. You can say that your natural affection for your brother led you into this.

ANNE. Is the alternative death?

KRUGER. In all probability.

ANNE. I choose death. (*There is silence for a moment as the witnesses of this scene look at one another and at* ANNE. KRUGER *draws himself up to make a speech, but* ANNE *forestalls him.*) Why delay? I have no desire to hear the speech you are about to make. My ideas are equally distasteful to you. Send me to face a firing squad now, while I am in the mood for it.

KRUGER. You don't know what you are saying. You see yourself as a heroine. But the people — the people your other brother died to serve — will not see it so. To them you are a betrayer of their cause.

ANNE. I have been loyal to the highest cause I know.

KRUGER. You have failed in the greatest loyalty of all — patriotism.

ANNE. Patriotism is not enough! Edith Cavell was right. There is a larger loyalty —

KRUGER. That will do! There is a limit to patience! Take her to the guard — (*Enter* ISABEL, *distracted.*)

ISABEL. Oh, Anne, Anne! I watched. I saw. I knew it would come out this way! (*She embraces* ANNE, *who does not return the affection.*)

KRUGER. So you were in this plot, too, Isabel? Will you add your confession to Anne's or tell us you knew nothing about it?

ISABEL. I'll take the blame — all of it. I knew she was impetuous and wanted to do it. I should have stopped her. I —

ANNE. She had nothing to do with it.

ISABEL. But Anne, I am not afraid — now that the thing is done — to share your punishment.

ANNE. You are too late. The deed is done. And I did it alone.

ISABEL. Don't repulse me, Anne. I can comfort you in sorrow even if I couldn't help you in danger.

ANNE. I'll die alone as I worked alone.

ISABEL. I shall not care to live when you are gone.

ANNE. You should have thought of that when you refused to help me when I needed you.

ISABEL. If I had another chance I'd not refuse. He was my brother as well as yours.

KRUGER. One of these girls has suddenly become a fool. The other was born one.

ISABEL. Perhaps we are foolish, Mr. Kruger. Our whole family gone — all but John. And it won't be long until he's caught, I suppose. How can I go on living without my sister?

KRUGER. If you are wise, you will disown her as a traitor.

ISABEL. Do you think your son will do that — he's engaged to her?

KRUGER. There are other girls.

ANNE (*for the first time near to tears*). You can take my life from me, but not my love. Herman will understand.

KRUGER. Lieutenant, take her back to the guardhouse! I'll have her confession typed immediately and sent over. See to it, Paula. (*Exit* LIEUTENANT *and* ANNE.) As for you, Isabel, I warn you that you shall be watched. We shall have no more trouble from your family.

ISABEL. I never felt like a revolutionist nor wanted to be one — till now! (*Exits.*)

PAULA. It is time to telephone any news for the daily broadcast, Mr. Kruger. (*Exits.*)

MISS LEE (*rising*). Well, Mr. Kruger, I can see where your troubles are not yet finished. The sooner you can make an example of that Anne Goodman, the better. After all, maybe you're lucky to have this happen *before* the wedding rather than after.

KRUGER. I'm sure of it. Thanks for these documents. When you have more data on this youth movement let me have it.

MISS LEE. I will. Give 'em hell, Mr. Kruger! The country's back of you! (*She goes out, saluting the flag on the way.* KRUGER *meditates; walks across the floor; gazes out the window; snaps his fingers; then shakes his head as if trying to shake off his doubts and goes back to the desk. There he picks up the telephone.*)

KRUGER. Give me our broadcast studio. — Hello, Bellamy? — Kruger speaking. Only one piece of news from this office for the government broadcast today, but it's important. Say that John Goodman, well known internationalist and leader of a pacifist youth movement who was arrested last night on a charge of treason, escaped today through the treachery of his sister, Anne. The government now has her in charge and will proceed with all possible speed to make an example of her, so that other obstructors to this war will know what to expect. Get that? Make it strong. The last chapter of this incident tomorrow. Nothing more today. (*As he puts the telephone down, his son,* HERMAN, *enters. He is twenty-six years of age and of fine physique. He is a more sensitive person than his father.* KRUGER *looks at him anxiously*) Well, son, that was a great article you had in the *World* last night.

HERMAN. I met Anne — in handcuffs and under guard — as I came in. What does it mean, father?

KRUGER. Sit down, Herman, and I will tell you. (HERMAN *sits in front of the desk,* KRUGER *behind it.*) You know I've been suspecting that her brother, John, was at the head of this youth movement. Yesterday I had him arrested. Today the evidence came from the secret service confirming all my suspicions and more. It is not only pacifist — it's traitorous. Anne knew all this and deliberately planned and executed John's escape.

HERMAN. What will happen to her?

KRUGER. She will be court-martialed and treated as an enemy of the country.

HERMAN. That means death.

KRUGER. Do you see anything else I could have done?

HERMAN (*slowly and cautiously*). You always do your duty as you see it.

KRUGER (*relieved*). That's a good boy, Herman. I knew I could depend on you. It's a hard blow, giving her up, but you'll get over that.

HERMAN. Let's not think of me just now, father. You want to do what's best for the country, don't you?

KRUGER. Of course.

HERMAN. And that's what I want.

KRUGER. Fine! I can't tell you how relieved I am, Herman. A man in my position has no privacy in his life. The public knows everything about him. If I preached " America first " and yet had as a daughter-in-law an internationalist — can you see what embarrassment it would cause?

HERMAN. Yes, I can see that. You want unity in your family as well as in the nation.

KRUGER (*settling back, satisfied*). Exactly.

HERMAN. But father —

KRUGER. Well?

HERMAN. Suppose there isn't unity in the nation in support of your policies?

KRUGER. What do you mean?

HERMAN. I hear many things that you don't. When you go about everyone applauds you and says pleasing things to you. But as a young reporter, I hear what men whisper. And the whisperings have been growing louder of late.

KRUGER. Of what nature?

HERMAN. Men are asking what's the good of all their sacrifice of blood and money in this war. The old ones are telling their disillusionments after the last war. The young ones — like John Goodman — are talking about doing away with nationalism altogether.

KRUGER. Forget it, son. It's just defeatist talk. It is heard in every war — always was, always will be.

HERMAN. Young Goodman had a larger following than you may know. Thousands of young people have made a sort of religion out of this thing. They look upon him almost as a messiah.

KRUGER. Romantic sentimentalism — nothing more.

HERMAN. But it has a powerful hold upon them. They will not take kindly to your arrest of John and even less kindly to the court-martialing of Anne.

KRUGER. What would you have me do?

HERMAN. It might be well to stop persecuting these young people and try to understand them.

KRUGER. To what end?

HERMAN. There may be something in their point of view.

KRUGER. Would you have me learn patriotism and wisdom for the conduct of my office by listening to visionary youngsters, to internationalists, to pacifists?

HERMAN. Don't be angry.

KRUGER (*with deep feeling*). I'm not angry, son. You don't realize how difficult a situation I am in. My duty directs me one way, my personal affections another.

HERMAN. I know. And your duty wins. I can understand that. But I am trying to say that you may be mistaken in your duty. You have been following one line of action because you thought it was best for America's future. So has the government as a whole. But it may not be best. It may, in the long run, prove our downfall.

KRUGER. Can patriotism ever bring our downfall?

HERMAN. There's a difference between patriotism and nationalism.

KRUGER. I see no difference.

HERMAN.   To love one's country — that is patriotism.   To give one's country supremacy over all other loyalties — that is nationalism.

KRUGER.   Son, let's not quibble over definitions.   I know this very clearly: my task is to help my country win this war. The time for arguments about that is long past.

HERMAN.   But suppose Goodman is right when he says that we shall have greater prosperity and happiness for our country in some sort of world federation of states on a live-and-let-live basis, rather than on this win-the-war-at-any-cost basis?

KRUGER.   This from you?   Have you been bitten by these serpents?

HERMAN.   I am only asking you to be open-minded and not inexorable.

KRUGER.   Don't fool yourself, Herman.   This is all rationalizing.   Down at the bottom of your heart you are really asking me to change a whole national policy in order that your fiancée may be spared.

HERMAN.   No, father, although she means more than life to me.

KRUGER.   I can't do it, son.

HERMAN.   I am thinking of you as well as of her.

KRUGER.   You needn't trouble.   I can think for myself.

HERMAN.   When I was younger you used to warn me against mistaking my stubbornness for thought.

KRUGER.   I never taught you to protect or plead for your country's enemies.

HERMAN.   Nor would I now.

KRUGER.   Are not John and Anne Goodman public enemies by their own confession?

HERMAN.   A large number of youth will say no to that.

KRUGER (*losing patience*).   Are the youth of the country telling me how I am to govern?

HERMAN.   They would like to help shape the world they will have to live in.

KRUGER. Neither they nor you will thwart me in the fulfillment of my duty.

HERMAN. Can't we make you see a new duty?

KRUGER. You are only trying to plead her case.

HERMAN. Not hers only. I am pleading for the right of everyone to put loyalty to his own conscience above his loyalty to the state.

KRUGER. My boy, it is hard for you, and for me — but you will have to adjust yourself to a world governed by facts, not sentiment.

HERMAN. You are determined that she shall die?

KRUGER. The country's welfare demands it.

HERMAN (*quietly, but with intense earnestness*). If she must die, she shall — but not alone.

KRUGER. Make no rash threats!

HERMAN (*rising*). It is no threat. It is a promise to free you and the country from one more rebellious youth.

KRUGER. You would not join that Goodman crowd?

HERMAN. I would.

KRUGER. Make no mistake about this. That movement must be stamped out. I must do it, even though I have to prosecute my own son.

HERMAN. You had better hurry your prosecution, then, for if Anne Goodman dies you will never see my face again! (*Exits. KRUGER paces the floor, distressed. But after a moment he squares his shoulders and reaches for the telephone. He speaks with determination.*)

KRUGER. Get Colonel Blakely at once. — Hello, Blakely? Kruger speaking. Get that confession? — When will the trial take place? — Why wait till tomorrow? — Yes, I have two reasons. I promised the public that the government would proceed in this case with all possible speed to make an example of such obstructors. That's one reason. The other is personal, but I don't mind telling you, colonel. You know my son was engaged to that girl. If he broods about her too long, he may do something sentimental. Not very likely, for he's a pretty level-headed boy. But the sooner it's all over and he can forget her the better. Understand? — At once? Good! Thanks! (*As he puts down the telephone,* PAULA *opens the door and leads in* DR. THOMPSON, *the blind preacher. His head is one that Michelangelo would have loved to sculpture, for it has strength and courage and rugged beauty in every line and in the waving mane of gray hair. He carries a cane with which he taps his way when someone is not leading him.*)

PAULA. Here's Doctor Thompson, Mr. Kruger. He's been waiting. (*Exits.*)

KRUGER (*shaking Thompson's hand and leading him to the chair* HERMAN *had vacated*). It's always pleasant to see you, old friend. And today, especially. Your help has been invaluable. Your influence in the churches has increased their efficiency as builders of morale.

THOMPSON. It's about that I've come, Thomas. You have been kind enough to ask my counsel several times since this fearful war began.

KRUGER. I've not gone wrong when I followed it. No one has a surer finger upon the public pulse than you. I'll testify to that before the world.

THOMPSON. And now I've come when you did not send for me to give you advice you did not ask. Will you receive it as kindly?

KRUGER. I hope so. What is it?

THOMPSON. The papers this morning carried a story to the effect that you are rounding up the leaders of the youth movement, and that you intend to make an example of them by having them charged with treason and then court-martialed. Is that true?

KRUGER. Every word of it.

THOMPSON. Then, Thomas, I've come to advise you to reverse that policy.

KRUGER (*startled*). Have you suddenly lost your senses?

THOMPSON. I've just begun to find them. I have supported this war and, as you say, influenced other people to do so because I have believed it to be a war of defense — defense of the principles of liberty and justice and of freedom of the individual's conscience from coercion by the state. This new policy is a denial of all these principles.

KRUGER. Our first duty, Doctor Thompson, is to win this war. If we don't win —

THOMPSON. What then?

KRUGER. Then none of your precious principles will be safe.

THOMPSON. I'm not so sure of that. But this I know: if we abandon those principles ourselves, there is nothing left to fight for.

KRUGER. But there is!

THOMPSON. What?

KRUGER. To win!

THOMPSON. Win what?

KRUGER. Victory! Supremacy!

THOMPSON. But victory for what? Supremacy for what?

KRUGER. For America! Isn't that enough? Surely you religious people are not so wanting in pride of your country that you do not wish to see her supreme.

THOMPSON. We are not striving to make America supreme. We are striving to make the kingdom of God supreme.

KRUGER. There's no difference so far as I am concerned.

THOMPSON. But there is a great difference. The kingdom of God is for all nations, not for America alone.

KRUGER. For our allies, perhaps. But for our enemies, too?

THOMPSON. Certainly. It is only because many of us have believed that the goals of our enemies were opposed to the kingdom of God that we have united to support America against them. But now as we see our government opposing our religious principles, we shall unite against it.

KRUGER (*sternly*). Dangerous words!

THOMPSON. But true, as you will certainly discover.

KRUGER.   In time of crisis our most cherished theories often have to be laid aside.

THOMPSON.   Not so! That is just the time to cling to them. If they won't work in time of crisis, they are no good!

KRUGER (*making a genuine effort at reconciliation*).   Come, come, Doctor Thompson. *We* are not going to quarrel. You use an older collection of words to express your ideas, but do we not mean the same?

THOMPSON.   I wish with all my heart that we did. But we do not. There are two ideas here. One is nationalism. It puts loyalty to the nation's supremacy as the highest virtue. That is your idea — am I right?

KRUGER.   That's it. What's wrong with it?

THOMPSON.   It's wrong because it produces bad fruit. It was the idea that dominated Napoleon and Bismarck and Cavour. They built up their own nations at the expense of all the others and left behind them untold misery, poverty, ruined cities, broken men. They sowed the seeds of the last world war.

KRUGER.   But how does your idea differ?

THOMPSON.   The other idea is the opposite of nationalism. It is the exaltation, not of one nation, but of humanity as the children of God. That's the difference, Thomas. You have come to the crossroads of these ideas, and you have started down the wrong road. Turn back, I pray you, and take the other one.

KRUGER.   I'm grateful for this lesson in history. But, Doctor, as you spoke I think I had an explanation of your change in attitude. May I be as frank with you as you have with me?

THOMPSON.   Of course.

KRUGER.   You religious people preach sacrifice, don't you?

THOMPSON.   We do.

KRUGER.   But you find it just as hard to practice it when the need comes as the rest of us.

THOMPSON.   What do you mean?

KRUGER.   John and Anne Goodman are members of your

church. They are your personal friends. You can't bear the thought of them being shot as traitors.

THOMPSON. John and Anne Goodman shot as traitors — did I hear aright?

KRUGER. John was arrested last night. Anne contrived his escape today. She will be court-martialed. Is probably being tried at this instant. She has already confessed.

THOMPSON. But this is alarming.

KRUGER. On the contrary, it should be reassuring. It means that the government has stopped trifling with the enemy within our borders.

THOMPSON. If Anne Goodman is executed, you and the government you represent will fall. It will be the beginning of a revolution.

KRUGER. I warn you not to let your anger mislead your tongue.

THOMPSON. I am not angry. I am frightened for you and for this country. All who care for the freedom of the human spirit will turn against you. You cannot win without them. Your own house will be desolated. Your son — if I know him truly — will die himself before he lets harm come to her. The nation you think you are serving will hold *you* the traitor and send your name down the centuries with a blacker stain than Benedict Arnold's. These things shall be unless you save that girl and completely change this damnable policy. I go now to start them. (*He turns and begins to tap his way toward the door.* KRUGER *sits speechless with a mounting fear. Suddenly* PAULA *bursts into the room.*)

PAULA. Mr. Kruger! They are going to execute her! Now! They found her guilty! From my window I just saw them marching her to the open space there. (*Going to the window*) There! There! From this window you can see! Oh, it's horrible — you can't let it go on! Do something, for God's sake!

THOMPSON. Yes, for God's sake! Act now if you would save her life and your own soul!

KRUGER (*reaching for the telephone, as* PAULA *stares in fascination of terror out the window*). Give me Colonel Blakely! Hurry!

PAULA. They've reached the spot!

KRUGER. Hurry, operator. (*He puts down the telephone, goes to the window and shouts. But the din of the city traffic drowns his voice, and he turns back to the telephone.*)

PAULA. They are standing her against that old wall.

KRUGER (*violently clicking the receiver*). Operator, if you don't get Colonel Blakely at once —

PAULA. They are tying a handkerchief about her eyes.

KRUGER. Hello! Hello! Why doesn't he answer!

PAULA. She tears it off.

KRUGER. Colonel Blakely? Not there? Where is he?

PAULA. A squad of soldiers is lining up. Oh hurry! O God, don't let them!

KRUGER. Get word to him immediately to stop the execution of Anne Goodman! Kruger speaking. Explain later. (*Frozen with fear, he stands holding the telephone and staring wildly in front of him.*)

PAULA. The officer is going to give the command. (*A whistle blows.*) What's that — there's a disturbance. Some civilians are fighting — trying to get through the guards. I see John Goodman — and your son, Herman, in front.

KRUGER. Not Herman! O God! Not Herman!

PAULA. They are breaking through! They are running toward Anne!

(*A volley of shots is heard.* PAULA *falls to her knees, sobbing hysterically.* KRUGER *sinks to his chair, his eyes wide with terror, as he grips his desk with both hands.* THOMPSON *stands trembling with apprehension, his face uplifted and his lips moving as in prayer. Moments pass. Slowly* PAULA *raises herself and looks again.*)

PAULA. She is still standing there! But someone is lying in front of her, the blood streaming from his head!

KRUGER. Not Herman! O God! Not Herman!

PAULA. The soldiers are lifting him up. They are carrying him this way. It's — it *is* Herman!

KRUGER. Herman! My son! What have I done to you!

THOMPSON. The revolution has already begun. I was too late.

KRUGER (*moaning in agony*). O Herman, what have I done to you?

THOMPSON (*stern as truth, but not unkindly*). Your son has chosen the better way. He has kept his country's name free from the stain your blind folly would have put upon it.

KRUGER (*unhearing*). O Herman, my son, my son!

CURTAIN

PRIZE MONEY*

by

Louis Wilson

CHARACTERS

LEMUEL JONES, *fifty-five, a farmer*
SADIE JONES, *forty-seven, his wife*
UNCLE PETE, *sixty-eight, Lemuel's uncle*
MARY SCHMIDT, *forty, wife of a neighboring farmer*
JENNIE SCHMIDT, *twelve, her daughter*

Scene: Living room in the home of Lemuel Jones, on a farm in central Illinois.
Time: The present.

PRIZE MONEY

The rising curtain allows us to look into the living room of the farm home of Lemuel Jones and his wife, Sadie. The walls are covered with fresh wallpaper gaily printed in a floral design. There are a few cheap prints in heavy gilt and plush frames and a gaudily lithographed calendar. At the left a door leading into the kitchen opens midway of the wall. Downstage from this door stands an old secretary desk, upstage a straight-backed kitchen chair. Downstage right is a window hung with freshly starched, ruffled white scrim curtains, and in front of it a small stand with a potted plant. Close beside is a rocking chair. Through the right wall upstage an open door protected by a screen leads into the yard. Against the rear wall is an old horsehair sofa, bumpy and worn. At right center is a reading table with a freshly laundered doily. The floor is carpeted by a large rag rug.

As the curtain rises we discover LEMUEL JONES *tilted back comfortably in a chair to the left of the table, his stockinged feet cocked squarely upon the doily. He is dressed in a blue work shirt and overalls.* LEMUEL *is a tall, thin, raw-boned man with a wiry shock of unruly, graying black hair. The deep furrows in his leathery face are somewhat softened by a several days' growth of iron-gray beard, a stubble which is stained about the corners of his mouth by a drizzle of tobacco juice. His features are neither unintelligent nor unkindly, but there broods over them an immense calm amounting almost to stolidity. He is reading a paper, and for a few moments there is no sound save the rustle of its pages. Then* SADIE *appears in the kitchen doorway and stands regarding him, her lips tightly compressed.* SADIE *is a tall and angular woman with faded yellow hair and*

*blue eyes. There is determination and enterprise about the set
of her mouth and a touch of color in her cheeks, but her shoulders are beginning to droop with the discouragement of many
years. She is neatly dressed in a clean but faded gingham house
dress.*

SADIE (*crossing to the table*). Lemuel Jones! Don't you
know I just got through cleanin' this house and that doily's
fresh ironed?

LEMUEL (*deliberately lowering his paper, then speaking in a
quiet, placating drawl*). I took my shoes off, Sadie. I warn't
hurtin' nothin'.

SADIE. Hmph! Don't suppose you'd have done *that* if it
hadn't been more comfortable. (*Jerking the doily out from
under his feet and holding it up accusingly*) Look at that! (*indicating a dirty smudge where Lemuel's feet had rested*).
Don't you know those old socks are full of dust out of the plow-
ing? You ain't changed 'em for a week. Oh dear. . . . (*Hysterically she crumples up the doily between her hands, walks
over to chair R. and sits down, her face averted from* LEMUEL *as
she stares unseeingly out of the window.*)

LEMUEL (*taking his feet down from the table, dropping his
paper on the floor, and putting on his shoes with methodical
slowness*). That ain't a-goin' to do no good. That little spot
wouldn't a-hurt it none to use nohow. (*For a moment there is
silence between the two while* LEMUEL *begins to lace his shoes and*
SADIE *continues to stare out of the window. Then* SADIE *turns.*)

SADIE. Lem, can't I have a fence around the yard this
spring? Them hens has begun scratchin' already around them
red piny bushes I set out last fall. You just can't have no
flowers at all without you have a fence.

LEMUEL. It'd make it awful unhandy a-gettin' to the house
with the milk pails, havin' to open a gate that a-way. Can't
you stick some stakes around your flowers so as the hens won't
scratch 'em?

SADIE. That's what you always say. You know it won't work. I ain't never had a decent yard like other folks.

LEMUEL. Well, we got to be kinda savin' on the money this year till we see how crops is goin' to be. Jim said this mornin' that Nellie wasn't gittin' no better. An' if she should drop off in one of them heart spells of hern there wouldn't be anybody left to take care of Uncle Pete but us.

SADIE. But Lem, we *can't* have him. Ain't I had enough to look after without takin' care of Uncle Pete?

LEMUEL. We'll have to if Nellie goes. Jim won't be able to batch and tend the farm and look after Uncle Pete too.

SADIE. Well, then he can get a girl to do the cookin' and watch Uncle Pete durin' the day.

LEMUEL. Jim ain't got no money to hire any help. You know that, Sadie.

SADIE (*with a sigh*). No, I guess he ain't. He's owin' the doctor now.

LEMUEL. An' Uncle Pete will be considerable expense to us when he gets them spells of hisn.

SADIE. I guess I don't have to have no flowers or nothin'. I guess maybe I wouldn't know how to act if I had any.

LEMUEL (*rising and making his way to the kitchen door, coal scuttle in hand*). I told Jim to bring him over if anything happened to Nellie. I'm goin' over to Jim's right now to get some more of that seed corn he said I could have. Maybe I can find some good pieces in that old roll of hog-wire for you to put around your flowers. I'll look when I come back.

SADIE. No, don't bother. That hog-wire don't do no good nohow. (LEMUEL *goes out through the kitchen door.* SADIE *rises, picks up Lem's scattered papers from the floor, pulls his chair over to the table and sits down, picking up some socks from a workbasket there and beginning to darn them. In a moment there is a knock on the frame of the screen door R. and* MRS. SCHMIDT *enters, calling out as she does so.*)

MRS. SCHMIDT. Hoo, hoo. . . . Anybody home? (MRS.

SCHMIDT *is a plump woman of medium height and ruddy complexion. Her good-natured, contented face looks out from under a sunbonnet which she removes as she enters. She is dressed in a neat gingham housedress. Close behind her is her twelve year old daughter,* JENNIE, *an unattractive, barefooted youngster, with freckled face and snub nose, whose red hair is bound tightly about her head in two encircling braids.*)

SADIE (*looks up listlessly*). Come in, Mary. Have a chair.

MRS. SCHMIDT (*taking chair R.*). Jennie brought your mail in out of the box. Give it to her, Jennie.

SADIE (*without real interest*). Any letters?

JENNIE. Naw, just some advertisin' things. There's printin' on the outside of the envelopes.

SADIE. Put them over on the desk, Jennie. I'll look at them after a while. (JENNIE *takes the letters to the secretary and then comes back to stand beside her mother.*)

MRS. SCHMIDT (*hitching her chair over beside the table and spreading out a woman's magazine*). I got a new pattern for one of them hooked rugs like Marthy Bascomb's been makin'. Got it from Fritz's mother when we was in town yesterday for Sunday dinner. There's a picture in here, and they've got some material all stamped like it down at the store. — Jennie! Quit lolling all over me like that. Can't you stand up yet? Go over and sit down on the sofa.

SADIE (*sorting out the colored comic supplement from Lem's paper*). Here, Jennie, is the funny paper. (JENNIE *takes the paper silently and starts toward the sofa.*)

MRS. SCHMIDT. Jennie! You come back here. What is it you say for the paper? Tell Mrs. Jones. (JENNIE *drops her head and squirms upon one foot.*) Well, has the cat got your tongue?

JENNIE (*almost inaudibly*). Thank you, Mrs. Jones.

SADIE. You're welcome, Jennie.

MRS. SCHMIDT. Now run along and don't be bothering people. (JENNIE *goes to L. and lies down upon her stomach on the floor, spreading the comic supplement flat before her. She props her head up on one hand and her bare legs wave in the air as she becomes absorbed in her reading.* MRS. SCHMIDT *continuing as she thumbs through the pages of the magazine*) There it is. See! That one in the middle of the page. Ain't that pretty?

SADIE (*leaning over to look but without enthusiasm*). Mhmm. It is pretty.

MRS. SCHMIDT. And there ain't a soul in the neighborhood got one like it, either. 'Tain't anything like Marthy's. An' I believe I like it better than hers, too. (*Noticing* JENNIE) Jennie! Git right up off that floor and pull your dress down. You should be ashamed, a girl of your age!

JENNIE. Aw, ma! There wasn't anybody lookin'. (*Reluctantly she gathers up her paper, draws up a chair beside the desk and sits there, continuing her reading.*)

MRS. SCHMIDT (*continuing*). Don't you think so?

SADIE (*bringing her wandering attention back with an effort*). Don't I think what?

MRS. SCHMIDT. Why, that it's prettier than Marthy's. My land! I don't believe you're half payin' attention. Don't you want to make one like it?

SADIE (*listlessly*). What's the use of tryin' to make anything pretty like that? I'm sick of doin' things to make the house look nice. Like as not Lem would come in and wipe his muddy boots all over it the next time it rained. (*With increasing bitterness*) I just about killed myself cleanin' this house. And now Lem's put his dirty feet up on top of this doily and it's got to go back into the wash. (*Throwing down her darning and rising*) I don't want anything only to get away from here. That's all I want — just to get away, an' never come back. (*Sitting down again and picking up her darning in despair*) But there ain't no use sayin' it, because I can't.

MRS. SCHMIDT (*leaning over the table and patting Sadie's hand*). I know. I've felt that way too, sometimes. A man just don't have the sense of a rabbit when it comes to things about the house. An' some of them's worse than others.

SADIE. It ain't just the house. It's everything he does. That's the reason Bill went off to Chicago just as soon as he could do for himself. He couldn't stand his pa's shiftlessness. But I just got to put up with it, that's all.

MRS. SCHMIDT (*to* JENNIE *who has laid aside the comic supplement and is busying herself with the contents of a little drawer of trinkets she has pulled out from the desk*). Jennie! *Will* you put that back where you got it? Do I have to send you home?

SADIE. Oh, let her be, Mary. She ain't doin' no harm with that drawer.

MRS. SCHMIDT. But my goodness, she's got to learn to have some manners. — Jennie! Do you hear me?

JENNIE (*pushing the drawer back into place unwillingly*). Well, I saw them funnies yesterday at grandma's. There ain't nothin' else to look at. Mrs. Jones, can I open your mail and look at that?

MRS. SCHMIDT. Jennie! For shame on you! What a thing to ask!

SADIE. It's all right, Mary. It's just advertisements. Sure. Go ahead, Jennie.

MRS. SCHMIDT. My! That girl! She makes me embarrassed every time I take her anywheres. She gets her manners from her pa. Fritz ain't got no company manners at all.

SADIE. Well, Lem ain't got *no* kind of manners. He just don't care. Last night right after I'd worked all day puttin' fresh paper on this room he scratched matches on the wall. There's marks all over the paper there by the kitchen door. If I'd just let everything go and live in a pigpen I guess then maybe he'd be satisfied!

MRS. SCHMIDT. Cheer up, Sadie. There's lots of women got it worse than you have. Just look at Lem's brother's wife now. Jim's every bit as bad as Lem, and there Nellie has him to put up with and Uncle Pete to take care of besides — and her with heart trouble. She ain't able to take care of things scarcely now, and no money to hire any help either.

SADIE. Well, I could go over and help her out some if she'd speak to me, and I would, too. But I ain't goin' where I ain't welcome. Nellie ain't spoke to me for two years, not since she didn't get elected into that Wednesday Afternoon Club and she thought I was the one that kept her out. (*Anxiously*) You don't really think she's likely to die, do you?

MRS. SCHMIDT. I dunno. I heard their ring on the phone last night. When their ring comes over the line I always listen in since Nellie ain't been feelin' so well. And it was the doctor callin' out.

SADIE. What did he say about her?

MRS. SCHMIDT. He just wanted to know how she was feelin'. But he called Jim down proper right there over the phone for lettin' her keep on doin' her housework. Said she'd ought to be in bed restin'. But land! I saw another washin' out on her line this mornin'.

SADIE. If she does drop off I guess I'll have to take care of Uncle Pete. There ain't no place else for him to go.

MRS. SCHMIDT. Sakes alive, you'll have a job! He can't move out of that wheel chair of his at all unless he has some help. An' he's gettin' so touchy nobody can live with him.

SADIE. Touchy? Uncle Pete's always made a pile of work for anybody to look after him, but he used to be right cheerful. Of course I ain't seen him since Nellie's been so huffy.

MRS. SCHMIDT. Yes, he did used to be. It was kind of pleasant to be around him because he was always seein' things that nobody else ever thought of seein' and showin' 'em to you, nice things like the colors in that potato patch of ours the day I was so tired pickin' up potatoes. (*With a half apologetic laugh*) I never seen nothin' pretty about a field of ripe potato tops before.

SADIE. I know. Uncle Pete never was like most folks. You

know he ran off to the city when he was only sixteen. They say he used to make his pa right out of sorts the way he hankered after books and pictures all the time. But what's come over him?

MRS. SCHMIDT. It's Nellie bein' sick, I guess. He's got to worryin' so because he's a burden on folks you can't say two words to him but he takes it right to heart. Thinks you're tryin' to hint about him bein' in the way.

SADIE. Poor fellow!

MRS. SCHMIDT. He's got so bad they won't let him have that little chest of his any more — you know, the one he keeps his curios in — not unless somebody's there to watch him. They're afraid he'll take that old pistol and kill himself maybe. There's a load in it and he won't let 'em take it out.

SADIE. Oh Mary! They don't think he'd do that!

MRS. SCHMIDT. That's what they're afraid of. I guess lots of them artist fellows commit suicide, don't they? You see things about it in the papers.

JENNIE (*who has been opening the mail a piece at a time and reading through a collection of catalogues and other advertisements, suddenly leaving her chair in great excitement and running over to the two women*). Mrs. Jones! Lookut! Lookut here! You got some money.

SADIE (*greedily, snatching the letter while the check falls upon the table to be pounced upon by* MRS. SCHMIDT). Money! Let me see.

MRS. SCHMIDT. My land! It's for twenty-five dollars!

SADIE. Honest?

MRS. SCHMIDT. It sure is.

JENNIE. It's from some bakin' powder people.

MRS. SCHMIDT. Bakin' powder? My sakes, I been bakin' with bakin' powder for twenty-three years an' they ain't never made me no presents.

SADIE. It's for a recipe. I won a prize. That's what it says here in the letter. See? (*holding out the letter*).

MRS. SCHMIDT. A prize! In that contest that was in the paper? What recipe did you send 'em?

SADIE. That economy cake like I made for the birthday party last month. It got third prize.

MRS. SCHMIDT. Well, don't that beat all? I bet if I'd have sent in my recipe for sour cream doughnuts I'd have got a prize too.

SADIE. No, it had to be something with bakin' powder in it.

MRS. SCHMIDT. Well, what's the difference? They're good doughnuts, ain't they? I've always made my doughnuts with sour cream and sody.

SADIE. I know, but they want recipes that'll help to sell their bakin' powder.

MRS. SCHMIDT. Oh! Them's mighty good doughnuts, though, even if I do say it as hadn't ought to. (*With a sigh of resignation*) Well, it's too late now, anyway. (*Taking new interest*) What you goin' to do with your prize money?

SADIE. Do? I'm goin' into town tomorrow an' buy myself a new hat. I been wantin' one for an age. An' then (*with reckless decision*) — an' then I'm goin' to drop a letter to Bill tellin' him to meet me at the train in Chicago next Saturday. That's just what I'm goin' to do. I been wantin' to go see my boy ever since he's been married, but I never had no money to go on before.

MRS. SCHMIDT. What's the sense of you goin' to Chicago? Your boy's comin' home to visit you this fall anyway. Why! You wouldn't have a cent left when you got back.

SADIE. I don't care if I don't. I'll have been away somewheres anyway. I don't care what happens when I get back. I ain't been more'n ten miles off this place for the last eight years and now I got the chance I'm goin' to go.

MRS. SCHMIDT. But sakes alive, Sadie, you can't go off visitin' in the spring when Lem's workin' in the field. Who's goin' to get his meals for him?

SADIE. Yes I can. I got my own money now an' I don't have

to ask *him*. I been gettin' his meals for the last twenty-five years an' it ain't goin' to hurt him none to get his own for a spell. I'm goin' off where I'll be company an' I'm goin' to *live* instead of all the time cookin' an' scrubbin' an' darnin' an' sittin' here in the evenin's watchin' Lem spittin' into the coal bucket.

MRS. SCHMIDT. I know. I know, Sadie. (*She sighs.*) Well, I like your spunk. I just hope you do. No one can say you ain't earned a vacation. (LEMUEL *enters R. and stands just inside the door.*)

LEMUEL. Sadie. (SADIE *turns, a bit startled.*) Sadie, Nellie dropped dead this mornin' when she was a-emptyin' out her wash water.

SADIE. Oh, Lem!

MRS. SCHMIDT (*rising*). Dead? Oh dear! Ain't that *terrible?* The doctor told Jim last night she oughtn't to do them things.

LEMUEL. I guess she was a-strainin' herself too hard a-liftin' them heavy tubs that a-way. She just keeled right over, Jim said.

MRS. SCHMIDT. Well, is there anybody there besides Jim and Uncle Pete?

LEMUEL. Yes, Maggie Niles come over from across the road. She's there now. I'm a-goin' right back to take Jim to town.

MRS. SCHMIDT (*stopping* LEM *as he starts toward the door*). Well, you just wait a minute and we'll ride back over with you. You want to go, don't you, Sadie?

SADIE (*somewhat dazed and matter-of-fact but without malice*). No, I don't know as I do. Nellie wouldn't speak to me while she was alive. I don't know as she'd want me around now if she had her say about it.

MRS. SCHMIDT. Well, you'll have to do as you feel, Sadie.

JENNIE. Kin I go, too, ma?

MRS. SCHMIDT. No, you'll just be in the way. You run on home and tell your pa when he comes in from the field.

LEMUEL. You can hold the screen door open for me, Jennie, while I wheel Uncle Pete in.

SADIE (*rising*). Uncle Pete? Lem, you didn't bring him over already?

LEMUEL. Why not? 'Taint no place for him to be over there.

SADIE. But I was goin' . . .

LEMUEL. Well, he's here now. Come on, Jennie, and hold this screen door open for me. (LEMUEL *steps out, followed by* JENNIE, *who pushes the screen door open wide and stands outside holding it so.*)

MRS. SCHMIDT (*crossing to* SADIE *and patting her shoulder*). I know just how you feel, Sadie. But it's the way things happen. And think of poor Nellie.

SADIE. Yes, but somehow I can't feel sorry for her *yet*. She's out of it all now. And I was goin' to get away from here for a while.

(LEMUEL *re-enters wheeling in* UNCLE PETE *whom he places in a position L. of table and facing front.* JENNIE *follows them into the room and seats herself on the sofa, an interested observer.* UNCLE PETE *is a frail, white-haired old man with a kindly, intelligent face. His high forehead, delicately modeled nostrils, mobile lips and keen blue eyes give an impression of essential youthfulness despite his evident feebleness of body. Although his features are basically strong the nervous playing of his slender fingers upon the comforter which covers his lap and his quick, appealing glances convey an air of hunted timidity, the mark of a sensitive soul being newly thrust upon the care of others from whom his welcome is in doubt.*)

LEMUEL. All right, Uncle Pete?

UNCLE PETE. Yes, quite all right.

LEMUEL. Then I'll go back out and bring in your things.

UNCLE PETE. Thank you, Lem. (LEMUEL *goes out R.*)

MRS. SCHMIDT. Oh, Uncle Pete, we are all so sorry.

UNCLE PETE (*quickly*). Not for me. It's Nellie. She had

a hard time of it. It was too much work, and taking care of me didn't help her any.

MRS. SCHMIDT. Oh, but you couldn't help that, and you was lots of company for her.

UNCLE PETE (*apologetically, to* SADIE). It was Lem made me come over here, Sadie. I didn't want to come in onto you without asking. Are you sure it's all right?

SADIE (*with evident hesitation*). I guess there wasn't anything for you to do but to come over here, Uncle Pete. They ain't no place else for you to go. (LEMUEL *re-enters with a suitcase and a small wooden chest. He piles them down by the sofa.*)

LEMUEL. Will you be all right, Uncle Pete? I got to get back over and go to town with Jim.

UNCLE PETE. Yes, I'll be all right. Go right along, Lem.

LEMUEL. Come along then, Mary. (LEMUEL *turns and goes out of door R.* MRS. SCHMIDT *starts to follow.*)

SADIE. Wait a minute, Mary. I'll go out as far as the hen house with you. Some of them fool hens has taken to eatin' eggs and I got to gather 'em a dozen times a day if I expect to get half of them. (*She steps out into the kitchen to reappear immediately with a small wooden grape basket in her hand.*)

MRS. SCHMIDT. Now, Jennie, you run right along home and be there to tell your pa like I told you.

JENNIE. Yes, in just a minute.

SADIE. I'll be right back in as soon as I gather the eggs, Uncle Pete. It won't take so very long.

UNCLE PETE. Take as long as you want to, Sadie. I'm not aiming to be any bother to you. (*The two women leave.* UNCLE PETE *remains staring front a moment, then turns and finds* JENNIE *watching him curiously.* UNCLE PETE, *with quiet but tragic conviction*) Sadie doesn't want me here, does she, Jennie?

JENNIE (*sitting down at the table opposite him*). Well, you see she was a-goin' off to visit in Chicago, Saturday. She won a prize. And now she can't go. I guess if you'd have waited till she got back she wouldn't have minded it so much. She said she didn't care what happened then.

UNCLE PETE (*reflectively*). Yes, I see. (*There is a moment's pause until Jennie's curiosity masters her.*)

JENNIE. Uncle Pete.

UNCLE PETE. Yes?

JENNIE. How did you get hurt that way? Ma won't ever let me ask you when she's around.

UNCLE PETE. I fell off a cliff, Jennie.

JENNIE. Well, what *is* a cliff? They ain't any cliffs around here, is they?

UNCLE PETE. No. A cliff is a high, rocky place. There aren't any around here.

JENNIE. Well, where was you then?

UNCLE PETE. That was by the sea. I was painting a picture.

JENNIE. Oh. (*There is another moment of silence.*) Uncle Pete.

UNCLE PETE. Yes?

JENNIE. What did you want to climb up onto that cliff to paint for?

UNCLE PETE. Because I loved the sea, Jennie, and I wanted to paint it from up there on the cliff. It was when I was up there that I could see its colors best.

JENNIE. Colors? The sea ain't got colors, has it? It's just a lot of water, ain't it?

UNCLE PETE. Myriads of colors! The sea and the sky and the earth — they are all alive with color.

JENNIE. But I ain't never seen any color in *water* — not unless it was muddy.

UNCLE PETE. Your eyes have never been taught to see. — But then you're too young to understand. You don't know what it means to love beauty until it hurts.

JENNIE. What hurts?

UNCLE PETE (*looking down at his slim, restless fingers,* JEN-

NIE *quite forgotten*). And now all I can do is to peel potatoes or darn socks while the world flames with beauty and my palette lies clean and my brushes dry in my chest.

JENNIE (*puzzled*). What you talkin' about? Why don't you paint pictures any more, Uncle Pete? I ain't never seen you paint none.

UNCLE PETE. People who live on charity don't ask others to buy them paints and canvas, Jennie.

JENNIE (*still puzzled*). Oh. (*Another moment of silence.*) Uncle Pete.

UNCLE PETE (*a trifle wearily*). Yes?

JENNIE. Why do artists shoot themselves?

UNCLE PETE (*startled*). Why, Jennie! What made you ask that?

JENNIE. Well, that's what ma told Mrs. Jones they did.

UNCLE PETE. Were they talking about me?

JENNIE. Uhuh. Well, *why?*

UNCLE PETE. You mustn't think about things like that, Jennie. They don't all shoot themselves. — But perhaps the real ones do.

JENNIE. What do you mean about the real ones?

UNCLE PETE. Nothing, Jennie. Nothing. I was talking to myself. (*A pause; then*) Would they let me go to the poor farm, do you suppose?

JENNIE (*horrified*). Why, Uncle Pete! Of course they wouldn't. That would look *awful*.

UNCLE PETE (*slowly*). Yes, I suppose that *is* the way they would feel. (*Another pause, then*) Jennie, will you do something for me, please?

JENNIE. Sure. What do you want?

UNCLE PETE. Put my things over here beside me. I don't think they are too heavy for you.

JENNIE (*boastingly as she brings the suitcase and drops it beside Uncle Pete's chair*). Of course they ain't. I can carry two full pails of milk at one time clear from our barn to the house without settin' 'em down once. (*Going back after the chest and lifting it*) This one's heavier than the other, though.

UNCLE PETE. Yes. Set it up here on the chair beside me.

JENNIE (*grunting as she lifts the chest to the chair*). There! Is there anything else?

UNCLE PETE. No, that's all. Thank you. And now perhaps you'd best go and tell your father as you promised.

JENNIE (*reluctant to leave*). But maybe he won't be in for a long time yet.

UNCLE PETE. But you promised your mother.

JENNIE. Well. They ain't anything else?

UNCLE PETE. No. Good-by, Jennie.

JENNIE. You don't want a drink of water or anything?

UNCLE PETE. No, thank you. Good-by.

JENNIE. Well then, good-by. I'll come back this afternoon maybe.

UNCLE PETE. All right. Good-by. (JENNIE *leaves.* UNCLE PETE, *to himself, with quiet conviction, as he opens the chest*) They don't want me, and there isn't any place else to go. (*Fondly he takes from the chest an artist's palette and a handful of brushes and sits brooding over them. Then, softly to himself, and nodding approval, he quotes*)

And those that were good shall be happy: they shall sit in a golden chair;

They shall splash at a ten-league canvas with brushes of comet's hair;

They shall find real saints to draw from — Magdalen, Peter and Paul;

They shall work for an age at a sitting, and never be tired at all!*

It would be *good* to be at work once more. (*He lays the palette and brushes back and draws out an old pistol. As he turns it*

* From *The Seven Seas,* by Rudyard Kipling. Reprinted by permission of Messrs. A. P. Watt and Son, agents, and Doubleday, Doran and Company, Inc.

over in his hands he shudders. Then, lifting his head, he gazes front and begins to repeat the poem again, softly and meditatively, but with increasing intensity of longing. SADIE *enters through the kitchen door, sees the pistol in his hand, and makes a sudden movement as if to go to him. Then she deliberately checks her impulse and stands, tense, near the door.* UNCLE PETE, *continuing*)

And only the Master shall praise us, and only the Master shall
    blame;

And no one shall work for money, and no one shall work for
    fame;

    (SADIE *leans forward listening in evident bewilderment, but makes no other move.*)

But each for the joy of the working, and each in his separate
    star

Shall draw the Thing as he sees It for the God of Things as
    They are!

    (*He looks down at the pistol in his hands and his grasp tightens upon it. He looks up again, tight-lipped and staring. His lips move and the words,* And they don't want me! *come low and tense. Staring at the pistol as if fascinated by it he begins slowly to raise it to his head.* SADIE *screams and rushes to his side.* UNCLE PETE *starts, his arm falls back and the pistol drops upon the floor. His head droops forward in despair and his hands clench upon the arms of the chair.* SADIE *throws herself on her knees by his chair.*)

SADIE. Oh, Uncle Pete! Thank God, I stopped you in time!

UNCLE PETE (*dully*). Why did you stop me? Now you'll have to keep me. And I wanted to go.

SADIE. Forgive me, Uncle Pete. I . . . I didn't ever think about you takin' it like that. I *didn't* make you as welcome as I ought. And I — I almost let you do it.

UNCLE PETE. Why, get up off your knees, Sadie! You couldn't help coming in just then, I suppose. But if you had only stayed outside a minute longer I could have been at work again.

SADIE (*rising, puzzled*). At work? But you tried to kill yourself.

UNCLE PETE (*wistfully*). Yes, at work again, painting with brushes of comet's hair. But now the seasons will pass, and my brushes will be dry. And I'll be living where I'm not wanted and waiting for the end that never comes.

SADIE (*struggling to understand*). But you couldn't paint if you was dead. What did it mean, that about — what you was sayin' when I come in?

UNCLE PETE. That was a poem about heaven, Sadie. I wouldn't have had the courage to have tried it if it hadn't been for that.

SADIE. Heaven? But — but they don't paint pictures in heaven, do they?

UNCLE PETE. If they didn't I guess it wouldn't be heaven for me.

SADIE. But if you want to paint pictures so bad, why don't you do it now? They ain't nobody to stop you, is there?

UNCLE PETE. It takes money to buy paints and canvas, Sadie, and I haven't had any money of my own for a long time.

SADIE. And you wouldn't ask for it?

UNCLE PETE. Would you?

SADIE (*fiercely*). No! I been wantin' to get off this farm an' go away some place for a visit for years. An' I guess I've earned it, too. But I ain't never had the money of my own, and I ain't beggin' Lem for it. If he can't give it to me of his own free will. . . . (*With sudden dawn of understanding*) Why, Uncle Pete, is that the way you been feelin' too?

UNCLE PETE. Yes, I guess that's about it; only I haven't even *earned* the things I get. I've just been a burden on folks.

SADIE. But you helped Nellie with the work around the house, didn't you?

UNCLE PETE. What I could do never amounted to much.

SADIE. Well, I guess that was more than Jim ever did for her. Most men don't seem to think a woman has any work to be helped with. (*Tentatively, after a pause*) Uncle Pete, can you buy paints and canvas out of the mail order catalogue?

UNCLE PETE. Sadie! I wasn't asking you to do that. I never intended anyone to know.

SADIE. But if I wanted to. . . . Tell me, can you?

UNCLE PETE. Yes, you can. I . . . I've looked at them there every year when the new catalogue would come. They're on page 1164.

SADIE. Do they cost much?

UNCLE PETE. Quite a bit, if you get enough to really work with.

SADIE. How much?

UNCLE PETE. Well, if I got everything I needed it would cost close to twenty-five dollars, but I could get enough to start on for ten.

SADIE. My! That's a lot of money for paint and canvas.

UNCLE PETE. Not paint and canvas, Sadie. It's for beauty and for dreams.

SADIE. For beauty and for dreams. Hmm . . . I never thought of it like that before. I looked at some oil paintings in a store once. I wanted one of them. It was awful pretty. It kinda made you feel good when you looked at it, like as if you was someplace else than where you was. But it was too expensive. — Uncle Pete, if I bought the paints and stuff for you, would you paint me a real picture I could hang on the wall?

UNCLE PETE (*incredulously*). You mean you'd really like to have one?

SADIE. Yes. I ain't never had nothin' like that, somethin' expensive that you owned just because it was pretty. Lem wouldn't see no sense to it.

UNCLE PETE (*his face shining*). Then I could *earn* the things you're going to buy for me. And I'm going to paint again. You don't know what that means to me, Sadie.

SADIE (*embarrassed*).   Why, Uncle Pete, that ain't nothin'
to fuss over.

UNCLE PETE.   You're too good to me.   (*There is a neighborly tap on the screen door and* MRS. SCHMIDT *enters.*)

MRS. SCHMIDT.   I just stopped in for a minute.   Lem brought
me back this far as he and Jim was startin' to town.   I got
something I want to tell you, Sadie.

SADIE.   What is that, Mary?

MRS. SCHMIDT.   I don't know why I didn't think of it sooner.
But you ain't aimin' to stay in Chicago much more than a week,
are you?   I got a spare bedroom.   I'll be glad to keep Uncle
Pete that long.   And then you can go just like you planned.

SADIE.   You really mean you would?

MRS. SCHMIDT.   Of course I do or else I wouldn't say so.
You write that letter to your boy.   I'm goin' in town this afternoon myself, and I'll mail it for you at the post office.

SADIE.   Oh, thank you, Mary.   That's awful good of you.
(*She hesitates and looks at* UNCLE PETE.)   But (*her assurance
growing*) — but I guess I've changed my mind about that trip.
I've decided I'd rather spend the money on some other things I
— I need more.

CURTAIN

PEACE I GIVE UNTO YOU*

by

Dorothy Clarke Wilson

CHARACTERS

JOSEPH, *a peasant*
MARTA, *his wife*
PETER ⎫
ALEC ⎭ *their two sons*
A SOLDIER

Scene: A peasant's cottage.
Time: A Christmas Eve.

PEACE I GIVE UNTO YOU

The one-room cottage of Joseph and Marta near the boundary of the tiny imaginary kingdom of Saxònia. At left (if desired, just behind the scenes) is a closed fireplace or built-in oven, with various cooking utensils hung on the wall. At center back is a table used for serving meals. At present there stands on this table a small evergreen tree adorned with tiny homemade candles. There are other candles about the room, and at least part of the light comes from these. There are several crude wooden chairs and against the wall at the right of the table a wooden bench. On the right is a door leading out of doors and in the rear, over the bench, a small window high in the wall. The place, though bare, is scrupulously neat.

MARTA *is discovered by the tree. She has just brought out of their hiding place two long, soft mufflers of bright-colored wool and two kerchiefs to wrap them in. With loving pride she holds them up, first one, then the other, and looks at them critically.*

MARTA. They are good — good. As good as the little grandmother ever made, and hers were the talk of the whole countryside. Never have I made such lovely ones, so fine and warm. (*She rolls them up in the kerchiefs, making a soft, bulky bundle of each, and places them in a conspicuous place in front of the tree. Then she rearranges the ornaments on the tree with painstaking care, standing off to view the effect. Finally, with a furtive glance toward the door, she reaches behind the tree and pulls out a similar package, also wrapped in a kerchief, which she unrolls, with frequent glances toward the door. Softly, holding up the muffler that it contains*) It's the nicest of all.

By far the softest wool and woven in the prettiest colors. But he'll never know. (*Suddenly she clutches it fiercely to her breast, dropping down in a chair by the table.*) Oh — Alec! Alec — my baby! (*At the sound of a footstep outside she jumps up and hastily rewraps the muffler, thrusting it back under the tree.* JOSEPH *enters, his arms full of fagots, which he places beside the fireplace. He moves heavily, and his shoulders are rounded from a lifetime of bending over the soil.*)

JOSEPH (*shivering and warming his hands at the fire*). It's cold tonight. (*Glancing at her sharply*) What's that you're doing, mother?

MARTA (*a little flustered, for she has just got the third muffler out of sight*). Just — just fixing the candles on the tree. (*She makes a pretense of straightening them.*) They get crooked. It's the heat of the fire, I guess.

JOSEPH (*suspiciously*). What you got in those bundles?

MARTA (*cheerfully*). Just some nice woolly comforters I made for you and — and Peter. I'll give you yours now. It'll keep you nice and warm when you're cutting wood this winter. (*She undoes one of the bundles, holds the muffler up triumphantly, and winds it around his neck.*) There! Isn't that nice and soft and warm?

JOSEPH (*deliberately removing it*). It's no time to be thinking of ·Christmas and all its trappings. We may not have a roof over our heads before morning. They're over the border already and not five miles away.

MARTA (*her hand flying in instinctive terror to her throat*). Not — not —

JOSEPH. Yes. Them. The enemy.

MARTA (*her hands dropping helplessly*). Then — that means — he won't be here. Peter won't be here.

JOSEPH (*tonelessly*). No. It wouldn't be safe for him to come — not now. It isn't safe for us, being here tonight. We ought to go back — away from the border.

MARTA. Why isn't it safe, father? Nobody would harm

anybody else tonight, not on Christmas Eve. Tomorrow is a holy day.

JOSEPH (*turning with a mirthless laugh to replenish the fire*). Christmas Eve! Holy day! When two brothers are hungry for each other's blood!

MARTA (*laying a quieting hand on his arm*). There, father, you mustn't talk so. You know our boys don't want to kill each other. They've just got things all twisted — somehow.

JOSEPH. They're twisted — all right.

MARTA (*suddenly eager*). You said they — the — the enemy, I mean — was only five miles away. Joseph, what if he were there with them tonight — my Alec?

JOSEPH (*whirling angrily*). Stop! Don't mention his name in my house. You'd be a traitor too if I'd let you.

MARTA. Alec isn't a traitor. He just —

JOSEPH. I know what he did. If it isn't being a traitor to run off and join the enemy's ranks and fight against your own kith and kin, I don't know what is.

MARTA. But — he was just a boy, and, after all, he's lived over there longer than he ever lived here. It's years since he's been over here across the line except for the long vacations and holy days. You sent him there yourself to school.

JOSEPH (*truculently*). So you're standing up for him, are you, and blaming me? Where's your patriotism?

MARTA. Is patriotism more important than — than loving? Hasn't a body got a right to love on Christmas Eve?

JOSEPH (*doggedly*). You still have Peter, haven't you? He's a son to be proud of, fighting for his country, working up to be a captain in the king's regiment.

MARTA (*sitting down, her hands folded helplessly in her lap*). Oh, dear, I can't understand it. Everything's messed up so. Alec's our son, isn't he, and every bit as good and brave as Peter, but just because he wears a different colored suit I can't even love him — not even on Christmas Eve. (*She suddenly lifts her head determinedly.*) I don't care. I do love him, and

I'm not going to stop just because some men are selfish enough to go fighting over a bit of land. And I've made a comforter for him just like Peter's, and it's going underneath the tree in plain sight, right where it belongs. (*With a defiant gesture* MARTA *pulls out the third bundle from its hiding place and places it beside Peter's.*) I'm going to light the candles, too! (*She takes one of the other candles and, with a hand that trembles from repressed emotion, lights the small tapers one by one. Then she takes a larger one and places it with determined fingers in the window.*)

JOSEPH (*sharply*). Here! What's that you're doing?

MARTA (*defensively*). It's just the Christmas candle. We always have it in the window. It's to light the way for the Christ child should he walk the earth tonight in the form of the beggar or the humble stranger.

JOSEPH (*angrily, trying to thrust himself by her to take the candle down*). Whoever walks tonight will take the form of spies and pickets. Quick! Let me put that out of sight and get the window covered!

MARTA (*patiently stopping him*). No, no. Can't you see, father? We've got to have it there tonight. The Christ child hasn't any part in all this fighting. What if he came — or — or Peter — and found the path all dark!

JOSEPH (*still protesting, but more feebly*). You'd have us murdered in our beds —

MARTA. Please — just tonight! (*Suddenly she crumples up in a chair, burying her face in her hands and sobbing.* JOSEPH *looks on a few moments helplessly, then pats her clumsily on the shoulder.*)

JOSEPH. There, there, mother! Don't cry. Don't cry. Maybe I spoke harshly. I didn't mean to.

MARTA (*sitting up and drying her eyes*). I — I miss them so. You don't know how I miss them, father. In the daytime when you're out in the woods, I think I hear them coming, and my heart beats so wild. I hear a noise, and I think it's my Peter whistling or my Alec throwing sand against the window. That's the way they always did when they came home. And now they're fighting — each other. Sometimes I think I can't bear it. (JOSEPH *pats her shoulder, then, blowing his nose to hide his emotion, goes over to the fire and warms his hands.*)

JOSEPH (*huskily*). It's going to be a cold Christmas — in more ways than one. I hope everybody has a warm bed.

(*There is a sound of whistling outside, coming steadily nearer.* MARTA *springs up, joyful and unbelieving.* JOSEPH *turns expectantly.*)

MARTA (*running to the door*). It's Peter. It is! It's my Peter! (*Before she can open it,* PETER *enters, closing the door quickly behind him. He is a tall, good-looking young man in a long military cape, high boots, and a captain's hat.* MARTA, *going toward him with outstretched arms*) Peter!

PETER (*leaning wearily against the door*). Well, I've got here at last. I'd have missed my way without the candle in the window.

JOSEPH (*eagerly*). Here, boy, here! Come over here by the fire and get warm. It's a night to make a wild boar shiver. Did you come far?

PETER (*laughing shortly*). Only from — the deepest hell. (*As* JOSEPH *starts to help him off with his cape*) No — I can't stay. I was a fool to come. They almost got me — out on that bare stretch between here and town.

MARTA. Got you? Oh, dear, you don't mean — they'd try to kill a body — not on Christmas Eve!

PETER (*ironically*). Oh, no. No — of course not! They were only shooting for the fun of it, and one of their bullets just happened to find my cap. It's a new way we've got of celebrating, that's all — celebrating the birthday of your Prince of Peace. (*Laughs bitterly.*) Good heavens above! How Somebody — somewhere — must be laughing at us!

JOSEPH (*sternly*). Shame on you, boy, for jesting. You're fighting for a great cause.

PETER. No doubt. If I could only find out what it is.

JOSEPH (*firmly*). You're fighting to save your country from the enemy. And we're proud of you, mother and me. You're all we've got left to be proud of since — since — (*His voice breaks.*)

MARTA (*hovering about anxiously*). Sit down, Peter, here by the fire where it's nice and warm. You won't be going back tonight?

PETER. I must. There's something big afoot. No knowing what will happen tomorrow. There's a rumor the enemy are planning a new attack.

MARTA (*protesting*). But tomorrow's Christmas.

PETER. Tomorrow is — tomorrow. (*He sinks into a chair with a sigh of content.*) You don't know how good it is to be home again.

MARTA (*suddenly bustling about over by the fire*). There, there! How stupid of me, to let you go all this time hungry! I'll get you some black bread and a bit of porridge.

PETER (*eagerly*). Are there pepper cakes?

MARTA (*happily*). Not only pepper cakes but lots of other Christmas goodies. You just wait —

PETER (*springing up, startled*). What — what was that?

JOSEPH. The frost cracking in the ground, most likely. A night like this it sounds like bullets snapping.

PETER (*backing away from the door*). Listen! It's someone coming. They've followed me here. I — I was a fool to come.

MARTA (*hopefully*). Perhaps — if we were real nice to them and offered them a bit of pepper cake — (*There is a sound of sand or small pebbles rattling against the window pane. Marta's face lights up with a wild joy. She runs and opens the door.*) It's Alec! It's my Alec! (PETER *stiffens, and his hand flies to his sword hilt. He stands very straight and stiff beside his chair.* JOSEPH *slowly rises and instinctively steps between* PETER *and the door.*) Look, father, look! It's Alec!

(ALEC *drags himself in. He is nearly exhausted, and his sol-*

dier's uniform is soiled and ragged. It is suggested that the color of Alec's be gray in contrast with the color of Peter's, which should be more striking, possibly a bright blue.)

ALEC (*smiling*). Hello, little mother. Merry — merry Christmas. (*He staggers slightly.*)

MARTA. There, there, baby! You're all tuckered out. Sit down here till you get your breath. (*She helps him to the bench.*) And how thin you are! I don't believe they've fed you very well.

ALEC (*weakly*). I've been sick.

MARTA. You don't need to tell me. Haven't I tended you through measles and whooping cough and I don't know what not? Bring a cup of water, father — quick — for Alec. (*JO-SEPH hesitates, then mechanically he fills a cup with water and brings it to MARTA. She gives it to ALEC to drink.*)

JOSEPH. You'd better tell him he can't be staying.

MARTA (*loosening his coat*). There! Don't that feel better?

JOSEPH. We haven't got any room in this house for traitors.

ALEC (*standing up weakly and facing him, eyes blazing*). I'm not a traitor. I'm fighting for the side that's in the right. This whole war's nothing but a selfish scheme of your petty weakling little monarch — (*Suddenly he catches sight of PETER, who at these words has drawn his sword half out of its sheath. Instinctively his own hand flies to his sword. He takes a step forward, and the two stand facing each other in undisguised hostility. After a pause*) You here — with our troops camped not an hour's march away! You've got more courage than I'd give you credit for. You Sacks are usually spineless creatures when it comes to fighting.

PETER (*slowly*). I ought to kill you.

ALEC (*indifferently*). Go ahead! It wouldn't be the first time I'd met a Sack singlehanded — and worsted him, too.

MARTA (*in keen distress*). Peter! Alec!

PETER (*hotly*). Do you realize you're talking to a captain of the king's regiment?

ALEC. Do you think I'd call any man captain who wore that uniform?

PETER. By heavens, that's enough of insult! (*His hand clenches on his sword, and he takes a step forward.*) A little more of this —

ALEC (*recklessly*). Come on! I'm ready. (*He grows suddenly dizzy and tries to steady himself.*) I — I — Where are you, mother? The room is swimming round and round.

MARTA (*pressing him back on the bench*). There, there! You mustn't try to talk. No wonder your head hurts with your brain all twisted up with queer ideas. Just sit there still, and I'll get you some black bread and a bit of porridge. There's some for Peter, too.

ALEC (*eagerly*). Are there pepper cakes?

MARTA. Enough to fill a basket. (*She sees* PETER *resolutely fastening his cape.*) Peter! You'll not be going now! We've still to have our Dedication Night together. Father, get the Book. It's lying ready on the shelf.

PETER. I've got to go. Surely you don't think I can stay here now — with him!

MARTA. Why not? Haven't we always had our Christmas eves together? (*She clasps her hands eagerly.*) It's just as I had dreamed — the tree all shining pretty, looking so peaceful in the candlelight — and just us four together, same as we used to be. I always loved the Night of Dedication. It seems for once as if heaven's no higher than a poor peasant's roof.

PETER. What matter whether it be a roof of boards or stars? There's just as much room beneath to hate and fight and — kill.

MARTA (*bustling about near the fire*). You'll feel different when you've broken bread together. Here, Peter, bring your chair up! I'll let you sit in your old places. It'll seem more natural and homey. Come, Alec. You'll both feel better to get a little warmth inside you.

PETER (*stopping her as she moves from the stove to the table and speaking in a low voice*). You're playing with fire, mother.

MARTA (*calmly keeping on with what she is doing*). Then who should know better than I how to handle it? For isn't the home built right around the hearthstone? (*She sets two bowls of porridge on the table, with a plate of black bread and one of pepper cakes between them.*)

PETER (*seizing her by the shoulders*). Mother — it's no use. Why can't you understand? Alec and I — we're strangers, enemies. We've sworn to destroy the things each stands for. We've sworn to kill — each other. It's monstrous, but it's war. It's the passion of hatred, and there's nothing stronger.

MARTA (*lifting her face bravely*). Love is a passion, too. And only the ages shall tell which is stronger.

PETER (*turning away with a shrug*). The ages — yes. It's too big for us to settle.

MARTA (*gently pushing him toward the chair at L. of table*). So we can just forget it all tonight, can't we? Sit down now, Peter. You can't tell me you're not hungry for some of your old mother's cooking. Is your head sort of steadied now, Alec? Why don't you give us a hand, father? Why do you stand there all turned to stone?

JOSEPH (*stolidly*). I'll not be giving victuals to an enemy.

MARTA (*patiently*). Nonsense! How queer you talk! When the good Book says "Love your enemies" just as plain as day! Sometimes I can't understand why folks are so afraid of a little bit of loving! (*She makes ALEC sit down in the chair at R. of table, gently but persistently pulling off his dirty coat.*) Sit right down, Alec. I'll be mending those tears in your coat while you eat.

JOSEPH (*stubbornly*). It's treason to give succor to the enemy. A loyal subject of the king — (MARTA *sews while the boys eat their porridge in silence.*)

MARTA. Kings are poor things to think about on Christmas

Eve. They seem so big and cold and far away, like the gold that jingles in their coffers. Christmas belongs to little things — to sweet fir trees and shining candles and soft warm bundles wrapped around with love. And that reminds me. I've made you each a nice warm comforter of fine combed wool and wrapped it in a pretty kerchief. (*She unwraps them and places one about each boy's neck, standing back in pleased fashion viewing the result.*) There! Aren't they fine and soft? The little grandmother herself never made better. They'll keep the wind out on these cold winter nights.

PETER (*significantly*). Aye, and maybe the bullets.

ALEC (*quickly*). 'Twill take more than a layer of wool to keep out our bullets. You Sacks will need hides bound with iron when we start battering your city's walls.

PETER (*half rising and fixing ominous eyes on* ALEC, *the muffler falling unnoticed to the floor*). Then you're really going to march against the city?

ALEC (*removing the muffler and smiling provocatively as he lays it on the table*). Ah, don't you wish you knew — and when — and how? 'Twould be a nice bit of gossip to run with to your frightened little king — unless you got one shot too many on the way.

MARTA (*anxiously*). Isn't the porridge good? It's flavored just the way you used to like it.

ALEC (*looking at his mother silently, then slowly turning to his bowl*). It's better than ambrosia, mother.

PETER (*with an obvious effort at self-control*). Aye, that it is.

ALEC. You dream about these pepper cakes nights when you're out lying in the mud.

PETER. With nothing in your stomach but a moldy crust.

ALEC. And nothing in your heart but homesickness and fear.

PETER (*wonderingly*). Then you have felt it, too? It's queer — our side and yours both feeling the same way. I wonder —

ALEC (*helping himself to another pepper cake*).   You wonder
what?

PETER.   Just why we're all so keen on fighting, after all.

ALEC.   You fellows ought to know. You started it.

PETER (*springing up furiously*).   You lie! An innocent, de-
fenseless people had their lands invaded.

ALEC (*shrugging*).   So that's the story they pulled off — to
make you fight. Oh, well, no matter — as long as it's started.

PETER (*angrily*).   And now it's started, we'll fight if need be
till our last drop of blood is drained.

ALEC.   Never fear. The last drop will be drained.

MARTA.   It's time we got the Book. (*Rises and puts aside
her sewing.*) I'll find the place. I can tell it by the picture.
(*She brings out a worn Bible and opens it.*) It's the one where
the shepherds are all gathered about the holy child. There's a
little young shepherd leaning up against an older one. We
named them Alec and Peter. (*The two boys continue to look
angrily at each other during the first part of Marta's speech,
then, slowly relaxing,* ALEC *goes to his mother's side.*)

ALEC (*looking over her shoulder*).   And there's a little lamb
somewhere down in a corner. See, there he is.

PETER (*joining* MARTA *and* ALEC).   And a smudge on the
angel's face where I handled it one day with dirty fingers. It
was the day before Alec got lost in the forest. I remember because I wondered if it was the angel taking vengeance on me
and taking away my little — my little brother.

ALEC (*soberly*).   I thought you were an angel when I saw
you coming. (*He goes back to his chair.*) Do you remember
the day we went hunting for the goats and climbed the hill
beyond the old stone bridge?

PETER (*his eyes kindling at the memory*).   And the storm
came up. Sure I remember. The snow came like a bunch of
fiends let loose. I've never seen the like. It's queer I didn't
petrify with fear.

ALEC.   If you were afraid you didn't show it. It's a wonder you didn't freeze to death using your coat to keep me warm. That was the second time you saved my life.

PETER (*returning to his chair*). Oh, that was nothing!

ALEC. From that day on you were my boyhood hero. You always looked so big and strong to me those days. (*The two brothers exchange a long look before* PETER *sits down.*)

PETER (*pensively*). Those — days —

MARTA (*pressing the Book into Joseph's hands and making him sit down near the light of a candle*). Read, father. It's open to the Night of Dedication chapter.

JOSEPH (*hesitating*). I — I'm not sure — Why, how your hands are trembling!

MARTA. Nonsense! It — it's the flickering of the candles. Read it, father, same as we've always done.

JOSEPH (*reading laboriously*). "Now there were in the same country" — Is that the place? (MARTA *nods serenely and sits down again to her sewing.* ALEC *munches a pepper cake, while* PETER *absent-mindedly crumbles his beside his plate.*) — "shepherds abiding in the fields, keeping watch over their flocks by night. And the angel of the Lord came upon them and the glory of the Lord shone round about them, and they were sore afraid."

MARTA. And no wonder, poor things. They didn't know then that the Lord likes best to pay visits to humble places.

JOSEPH. "And the angel said unto them, 'Fear not, for behold I bring you good tidings of great joy which shall be to all people.'"

MARTA. Now this is the part we all say together. (*She starts repeating with* JOSEPH *as he reads, then* ALEC *chimes in, finally* PETER.)

JOSEPH. "'For unto you is born this day in the city of David a saviour which is Christ the Lord. And this shall be a sign unto you. Ye shall find the babe wrapped in swaddling clothes and lying in a manger.'"

MARTA. Which maybe meant nothing more nor less than a poor peasant's cottage.

JOSEPH. "And suddenly — " (*He pauses, then springs up.*) Hark! What was that? (*There is a sound of footsteps outside, and a loud beating on the door.* JOSEPH, *rising and standing against the door*) Who — who's there? (ALEC *and* PETER *both rise and stand looking apprehensively toward the door.*)

SOLDIER (*speaking in a loud voice outside*). Don't be afraid. We aren't going to harm you, and we don't want to come in. Only you've got a Sack there hidden, and we know it. One of our scouts saw him enter your house not an hour ago. He got a glimpse of his officer's uniform, plain as day. You give him up right off, and we won't make any trouble. But we aren't letting any Sacks leave this place alive tonight. Understand?

JOSEPH (*falteringly*). Yes — yes. I understand.

MARTA (*in a terrified whisper*). He wants — Peter. He wants — my Peter. (PETER *stands as if turned to stone. He lifts one hand slowly to his forehead, then drops it heavily.*)

PETER. Tell him — I'll come.

SOLDIER. There's no use resisting. We've got soldiers planted in the woods, so you can't possibly get away without our seeing. I'm going there now and wait. If he's not out of the house in ten minutes, there'll be no house. Understand?

JOSEPH. I — understand. (*He turns and faces the rest, misery in his eyes. There is a long silence. Suddenly* ALEC *walks across the room and faces his brother.*)

ALEC (*in a low, commanding voice*). Take off your cape!

PETER. I — I — What did you say?

ALEC (*summarily*). Take off your cape.

PETER. They're going to kill me. I — I'm not ready to die.

ALEC. Take off your cape! (*Hardly conscious of what he is doing,* PETER *takes off his cape, disclosing his simple soldier's uniform beneath.* ALEC *puts the cape on over his own uniform, removing his sword and placing it on the table.*)

PETER (*dazedly*). What are you doing?

ALEC. No matter. Now — give me your hat and sword.

Quick! We've no time to waste. (*As* PETER *is too dazed to obey,* ALEC *tears them off and puts them on himself.*)

PETER (*springing forward*). No — no! In heaven's name, not — *that!*

ALEC. Quiet! They'll hear. (*For a moment they struggle together, then* ALEC *succeeds in pinning Peter's hands behind him.*)

JOSEPH (*attempting to intervene*). What — I can't let you —

ALEC (*sternly*). Be quiet! Do you want that fellow back again! (*Gently but firmly he presses* PETER *back into the chair by the table.*)

PETER (*still struggling*). Alec — you mustn't — (*Suddenly his head slumps forward on his arms.*)

ALEC (*bending over him and speaking in a commanding voice*). Listen! (*Choosing his words slowly and carefully*) I don't mind going — not this way. It's easier for me than you. I've not so much to leave. And I've been face to face with death before. I may be nearer ready. Besides, I've got a notion — I'd rather give myself for love than hate — tonight. It — it's more the stuff that holy nights like this are made for. And somehow — all at once — there's nothing else that seems to matter. (*He starts toward the door. All at once he flings back his head, something like the triumph of adventure in his eyes.*) It will be a little glorious, I think! Just one brief flash — And heaven is just above a peasant's roof. (*He turns suddenly to* MARTA) I'd like my comforter —

MARTA (*her voice breaking as she winds it around his neck*). My darling — it will keep you nice and warm. (*He stoops and kisses her.*)

ALEC (*gently*). Hatred or — love. You're right, little mother. The ages shall tell which is stronger. Yet — the truth of ages was once revealed in a single holy night.

MARTA (*brokenly, yet with a strange exaltation*). My Alec

— my boys — (PETER *lifts a haggard face and, as if suddenly conscious of what he is doing, springs to his feet.*)

PETER (*flinging himself across the room toward* ALEC). No — no! What am I thinking of! Quick, Alec! Quick! Give me back my cape. Do you think I'd let you — die — for me, when I would gladly give my life for you! I've always loved you better than myself.

ALEC (*looking into his brother's eyes with deep emotion*). We've loved each other.

PETER. What fools we were to think we could be enemies!

ALEC (*in sudden passion*). What fools men are to fight! (*There is a step outside the door. The brothers spring to attention.*)

JOSEPH (*hoarsely*). He's coming back. May God — have mercy on us! (*There is a knock at the door.*)

ALEC (*in a low, commanding voice*). Quick! Let me go!

PETER. No, no! I can't!

MARTA (*moving toward the door*). I'll go and let him in. He may be cold.

JOSEPH. Mother — you're mad! (*She quietly takes a candle and goes and opens the door, holding the candle high.*)

MARTA. There, there, come in! I don't know who you are — but may the peace of God and his holy night be with you. (*The* SOLDIER *enters awkwardly. He wears a uniform like the one* ALEC *wore at first. It is worn and bedraggled.*) My sakes, you're nothing but a boy! And all your clothes are soaked! Come over by the fire and get warm.

PETER (*warningly, his hand closing over the sword*). Mother — keep out of this! This is a job for men — and men alone — to settle.

SOLDIER (*earnestly*). Don't — don't look at me like that! I haven't come to kill you. We found we couldn't — not tonight. We'd forgotten what day it was. We've been talking about it outside — it made us think, seeing your candle in the window.

There are candles — somewhere over there — for us. And all at once it made this war seem pretty small. (*Turning help-lessly to* MARTA, *who alone seems to catch the meaning of his words*) You — you understand?

MARTA. Of course! How many are there of you out there in the cold?

SOLDIER. Only a handful. About half a dozen. We'll go away. I promise — we'll not bother you again. (*With sudden passion*) Men must be fools to think they ought to fight on Christmas Eve!

PETER (*suddenly relaxing his tension*). Men must be fools to think they ought to fight — at all!

ALEC (*passionately*). Then why — in God's name — don't we stop it! (*All three stand looking at one another in silence, the vision stirring a strange excitement in each.*)

SOLDIER (*suddenly clasping Peter's hand*). 'Twill be the biggest war we ever fought —

MARTA (*laying a gentle hand on the soldier's arm*). Go out and bring them in. We'll have our Dedication Night together. There's lots of porridge and black bread and Christmas goodies — just as if you were at home.

SOLDIER (*eagerly*). Are — are there pepper cakes?

MARTA (*bustling about happily*). Enough and to spare. Now run along.

SOLDIER (*still unbelievingly*). You really mean it?

MARTA. Of course. You think they will not understand? Then tell them — tell them a mother's waiting for them, and it's Christmas Eve. (*The* SOLDIER *gives her a wondering, almost worshipful look.*)

SOLDIER. We'll be right back. (*He goes out.*)

MARTA. Put a fresh log on the fire, Peter. They'll be cold and wet. And, Alec — take off that sword. You'll not be need-ing it tonight, thank God. And, father! While he's gone, why don't you finish up our chapter? (PETER *puts a fresh log on the fire.*   ALEC *removes the cape and sword.*   JOSEPH *fumbles for the place in the Book which he still holds in his hand.*)

JOSEPH (*his voice rising strong and triumphant*).   " And — and suddenly there was with the angel a multitude of the heavenly host praising God and saying, ' Glory to God in the highest and on earth peace — and on earth — *peace* —' "

CURTAIN

THE TAIL OF THE DRAGON*

by

Elliot Field

(

CHARACTERS

LIU WEN-CHIN, *a merchant*
LIU-WONG SOONG-YUN, *his wife*
LIU MING-KWAN, *their son*
KING CHI-KWEI, *a broker*
KONG SU, *a maid*

Scene: The parlor of the Liu home in Shanghai.
Time: The present.

THE TAIL OF THE DRAGON

Entrance doors at right and left, slightly upstage. Only the minimum properties are needed to represent a typical parlor or reception room in the home of a well-to-do Chinese family. A long, narrow table against the center of the rear wall, upon which stands an incense burner midway between two candle-sticks. A panel-picture of a dragon hangs in the exact center of the rear wall, with a scroll on either side, symmetrically placed. Directly in front of the long table is a small, square table, flanked on either side by straight-backed chairs. If desired, straight-backed chairs may be placed against the rear wall on either side of the long table. Against the side walls, down from the doors, are small tea tables, likewise flanked by straight-backed chairs. Scrolls or painted panels are hung on the side walls directly over the tea tables. If there is a rug on the floor, it should simulate richness. Other touches may be added as desired, such as hangings, potted plants, red chair cushions, etc.

Chinese furniture is made from teak or from redwood; red cedar or mahogany would simulate the latter. Bamboo is used occasionally for lighter pieces and for chairs. The long table is usually higher than the square table, and is ordinarily without a cover. The square table (3 to 3½ feet) is empty save for the letters required in the play. The candlesticks, often of pewter, may be either empty or fitted with red candles. In place of the brass incense burner an ordinary medium-size brass jardiniere could be used. If it is desired to show the customary ancestral tablet, this could be fashioned of wood, varying from two to five feet in height, in red with gold trim and gold lettering. Its place is on the long table, often in a small shrine, against the wall or on a shelf above the table.

MR. LIU *is seated R. of the square table, reading a letter. He frowns as he reads and further betrays vexation by drumming his fingers on the table, alternating this with the twisting of a button on his waist-length jacket. Enter* MRS. LIU *L. She stops near the door and regards her husband anxiously.*

MRS. LIU. You are disturbed, Wen-chin.

MR. LIU. And with excellent reason. (*He taps the letter.*) Ming-kwan has at last condescended to take time from his absorbing duties at the college and write to his humble parent.

MRS. LIU (*approaching the table*). But why are you vexed? Ming-kwan must be very busy with his studies. Surely a letter from him should be a matter for rejoicing. Is it not an evidence of his filial respect?

MR. LIU. It seems that filial respect is one of the least of our son's virtues.

MRS. LIU. What can you mean, father?

MR. LIU. It has turned out exactly as I feared. When Ming-kwan insisted on entering this college instead of following my preference and going into the dry fruit business with me, I still had the hope that he would select some courses that would fit him to take his place at my side and help me to combat the financial misfortunes that are crowding fast upon our family. Now he writes me that he is studying (*he consults the letter*) — sociology.

MRS. LIU (*sitting opposite him*). What is that? Is it — dangerous?

MR. LIU. If it is useless, it is dangerous, Soong-yun. They study the most ridiculous matters in those colleges. If I must part with all this money for my son's education, I have a right to expect that he will be sensible and prudent.

MRS. LIU. But perhaps he can earn a living at this so — so — (*She pauses, helplessly*).

MR. LIU (*glancing down at the letter*). Sociology. If you think so, allow me to read you more of our son's nonsense. (*Reads*) "It is my ambition to help China, to work for her

freedom from foreign oppressors, to give my life to righting the
social and industrial wrongs that hinder her progress, to be a
true patriot. I have joined a little band who call themselves
'Enlightened Sons of China.' We pledge ourselves to work for
popular education and for the relief of all who are oppressed.
We speak at street meetings and visit the factories to learn the
condition of the workingman. We even go out into the villages
and teach the people how to read the modern writing." Modern
writing! Hah! (*He slaps the letter down on the table.*)

MRS. LIU (*innocently*). It should please you, father, to think
that our son is so active and useful. (MR. LIU *rises and begins
pacing to and fro.* MRS. LIU *rises also and remains standing
beside the table.*)

MR. LIU. Please me! Our son active and useful! (*He stops
and glares at her.*) Do you realize that our son may be a
communist?

MRS. LIU (*dubiously*). Is it wicked to be a communist?

MR. LIU (*resuming his pacing*). Worse than that. It is
foolish. It is likely to land him in jail. (MRS. LIU *gives a little
squeal of fright.*)

MRS. LIU. What are you saying, father!

MR. LIU. And for another, it will not earn him one single
cash.

MRS. LIU. But he must not go to jail. We must stop it.

MR. LIU. Still more. (*He stops and looks keenly at* MRS.
LIU.) From Ming-kwan's letters, I gather that he is becoming
very much interested in Christianity. He speaks of going to
meetings and study classes and of his talks with a certain professor whom he admires exceedingly.

MRS. LIU (*alarmed*). He would not do that! He has too
much filial regard for his family.

MR. LIU (*with a mocking laugh*). I have already told you
that filial piety is one of the least of our son's virtues.

MRS. LIU. You misjudge Ming-kwan. He is a dutiful son.

MR. LIU. You think so? Then listen to this — I have saved

the worst until the last. (*He picks up a newspaper clipping from the table.*) The title of this article is " Chinese Parents " and it was written by — Ming-kwan.

MRS. LIU (*clasping her hands*). By our son? That is splendid!

MR. LIU. Wait until you have heard what it says and then consider if our son has left a shred of filial piety. (*Reads*) " The Chinese home is a territory governed and controlled by parents, with their children as subjects. Nearly every Chinese father thinks that he himself is the creator and treats his children as his creatures. Of course parents have the duty to educate their children, but they have no right to use them as if they were their property." (*Holds out the clipping.*) Our most filial son!

MRS. LIU (*aghast*). Ming-kwan wrote — that?

MR. LIU. He did. It is well that it has been called to my attention. It will enable me to take the proper steps before it is too late.

MRS. LIU (*alarmed*). What are you going to do?

MR. LIU (*picking up a sheet of paper*). Here is a copy of the letter I have sent him, telling him that I have read his worthless article, and that, according to it, he does not even recognize me as his father. That in consequence it would be quite just and proper for me to refuse to recognize him as a son. (MRS. LIU *gasps.*) I ordered him to return here at once. (*Folds up paper.*) My letter was delivered to Ming-kwan yesterday. I expect him home today. (MR. LIU *sits by the table, drumming on the top with his fingers. A pause.* MRS. LIU *stares at him.*)

MRS. LIU. What will you say to Ming-kwan?

MR. LIU. I shall, of course, demand an explanation of this shameless article of his. I am now convinced that for his own good I must take him away from that college. Moreover, it will give me an excellent reason to require his obedience to our arrangement with Mr. King.

MRS. LIU.   Is it possible that these modern ideas of his will lead him to (*she hesitates*) — to refuse?

MR. LIU.   That will not influence me.

MRS. LIU.   But suppose there is someone else whom he —

MR. LIU.   He must yield to our wishes. Am I not his father, and are you not his mother? There is still another reason why our son must not refuse to recognize his filial duty to his family. Sit down while we discuss it. (*She sits opposite him.*) I have requested from Mr. King the loan of a considerable sum of money.

MRS. LIU.   To help you with your business?

MR. LIU.   Precisely. The market for dry fruits is not what it used to be. Our country is torn with war and dissension, and there are many others who are in financial difficulty. My business is in such a condition that it is absolutely necessary for me to secure some money. So, you see, nothing must happen to cause Mr. King to change his mind.

MRS. LIU.   Has he not agreed to the loan and is not the security satisfactory?

MR. LIU.   The security that I offer is entirely satisfactory to Mr. King. Moreover, he has assured me that if our two families are united and Ming-kwan comes home to enter the business with me, he himself will see that any further necessary funds will be provided.

MRS. LIU.   But I do not understand. What could happen to cause Mr. King to change his mind about lending you the money?

MR. LIU (*leaning across the table*).   We must be certain that Ming-kwan consents to marry King Chen-shu. (MRS. LIU *stares at him a moment as if to be certain of his meaning.*)

MRS. LIU.   Are you saying that — that if our son refuses to marry Mr. King's daughter, Mr. King might refuse to give you the money?

MR. LIU.   I am saying precisely that.

MRS. LIU (*spreading out her hands*).   Surely Mr. King

would not make such a condition. He knows the proprieties. He would lose face. (MR. LIU *shrugs his shoulders and leans back in his chair.*)

MR. LIU. Mr. King is abundantly able to make his meanings clear without losing face. It is true that he named no such condition, but I could hear the hissing of the serpents in his courteous words. Alliance with our family seems to mean much to Mr. King Chi-kwei. He quite evidently has set his heart upon it, and so, I firmly believe, has Chen-shu also. From the hints that Mr. King has dropped, I surmise that his daughter has already smiled upon Ming-kwan.

MRS. LIU (*with a sigh*). I only hope that Ming-kwan will desire what we desire for him.

MR. LIU (*frowning*). Nothing must be left undone to make certain that Ming-kwan will act like a filial son. Mr. King is coming here this afternoon to complete the final arrangements for the loan and if I am not able to assure him of our son's consent to this marriage, it is altogether probable that (*he spreads out his hands*) — well, unexpected difficulties will arise. Mr. King will delay giving me the money, and I shall be financially ruined.

MRS. LIU (*gasping*). Ruined? Wen-chin!

MR. LIU (*with a gesture of resignation*). Yes, ruined. Is it not clear to you now why Ming-kwan must obey?

MRS. LIU. But if you talk persuasively to Ming-kwan, if you are gentle, he may —

MR. LIU. Gentle! (*Drawing himself up*) I shall carefully set forth the reasons. That much I am willing to do. But — Ming-kwan must obey. (*Enter* KONG SU R.)

MRS. LIU. Yet I beg of you, father, that you — (*She pauses and indicates to* MR. LIU *the presence of* KONG SU.)

KONG SU. Madam.

MRS. LIU. What is it, Kong Su?

KONG SU. Mr. King Chi-kwei is calling. (MRS. LIU *glances inquiringly at* MR. LIU.)

MR. LIU. Show Mr. King in. (*Exit* KONG SU *R.* MR. LIU *rises.* MRS. LIU *immediately does the same.*) If Ming-kwan arrives while Mr. King and I are conferring, you will have opportunity to converse with him. Be sure to admonish him that we are confidently expecting that he will act like a filial son in all things.

MRS. LIU. I shall do as you request. May you be given wisdom in your interview with Mr. King.

MR. LIU. I shall conduct the conversation astutely.

(*Enter* KING CHI-KWEI, *followed by* KONG SU, *R. He pauses just inside the door and gives the handshake — right palm over left, right thumb covering left thumb, with a slight up-and-down motion — bowing meantime.* MR. *and* MRS. LIU *return the salutation. Exit* KONG SU *R.*)

MR. LIU. We trust you are quite well.

KING. I am in abundant health and hope you both are the same.

MR. LIU. We are happy to have you in our home.

KING. I am indeed grateful for the privilege.

MR. LIU. It will give me much pleasure if you will accompany me to my private room, where we can talk quite uninterrupted.

KING. It will give me serene pleasure.

MRS. LIU (*to* MR. KING). Please feel at home. (*She exits R.*)

MR. LIU. You are experiencing no difficulty in making the necessary business arrangements?

KING. So far all has gone well. I anticipate a most successful conclusion to our negotiations. I am humbly grateful to be able to be of service to you. You are expecting your son?

MR. LIU. You are most kind. I expect Ming-kwan at any hour.

KING. It is indeed fortunate that you and I are to become relatives. I am greatly honored.

MR. LIU. It is I who am honored. On Ming-kwan's return it will give me pleasure to inform him of the great happiness that is in store for him. I rejoice that he is a most filial son.

KING. I am profoundly grateful that my daughter is to live under your roof.

MR. LIU. We shall welcome her with delight. (*With a gesture toward L.*) Shall we proceed within?

KING (*bowing*). I await your word. (*They exit L. KONG SU enters R. with two handleless cups and some delicacies on a tea tray, crosses over and exits L. Enter MRS. LIU R. She comes over to the table and stands looking down at the letters. She sits R. of table, picks up one of the letters and examines it curiously. As KONG SU enters L. carrying the empty tea tray, MRS. LIU looks up from the letter and her eyes follow KONG SU speculatively.*)

MRS. LIU. Kong Su.

KONG SU (*turns and stands respectfully waiting*). Madam?

MRS. LIU. When Ming-kwan arrives, send him at once to me —here. (*KONG SU bows and exits R. MRS. LIU rises, goes over to the door L. and looks out. The murmur of men's voices is heard outside L. MRS. LIU, shaking her head as if to express doubt and concern, returns slowly to the table and stands staring down at the letters. She sinks into the chair R., folds her hands idly in her lap, and gazes meditatively up and out. She again shakes her head and bends over the letters. She picks up one of them, turns it this way and that, and starts to read with a laborious following of the characters with her forefinger and with much puckering of her brows. It is very apparent that the contents of the letter disturb her, for she looks up several times with a frown and shakes her head. She gives a sudden start and half rises from the chair, looking anxiously out L. Apparently satisfied that no one is coming, she sinks back into the chair and bends over the letter again. Enter MING-KWAN R. He stops just inside the door, unseen by his mother, and observes her a moment with smiling interest. His gaze then roves the room and rests finally upon the altar table. He steps noiselessly toward it, scans it half wistfully and with a soundless sigh gives an expressive gesture of hands and head meant to convey a suggestion of his inward conflict. His smile returns as he looks again*)

*at his mother. Stealing up behind her, he looks down over her
shoulder and then steps back several paces.*)

MING-KWAN. Mother! (*She gasps and turns quickly.*)
Would you like to have a reading — by the author? (MRS. LIU
lays the letters on the table and shakes her head reprovingly.)

MRS. LIU. Ming-kwan! I am rejoiced that you have come
again. But you must not steal up on me unawares. Or (*she
holds up a warning finger*) — I won't tell you any more stories
of the olden days.

MING-KWAN (*pretending dismay*). But I must hear about
the bridge of pretty maidens and the river of heaven, or the
story of Chang and the dragon-tiger mountain of Kiangsi. I
came home just for that. (*She looks up at him with a tender
smile. He is standing at her side, his hand affectionately on her
shoulder.*)

MRS. LIU. Many, many years ago, a weaving girl married a
herdsman. They were so happy together and enjoyed each
other's company so much that they neglected their several duties.
So the Lord of Heaven, the father of the weaving girl, separated
the couple, placing one on one side of the river of heaven and
one on the other. Thus they were warned not to fail in the
performance of their rightful duties. It came to pass that —

MING-KWAN (*interrupting*). I know the rest, mother. (*He
walks slowly around to the other side of the table.*) Why did you
choose that particular one?

MRS. LIU (*glancing sidewise at him*). Surely the simple story
of the herdsman and the weaver will not rob you of your smile,
my son.

MING-KWAN. Yes, the simple story of the age-long struggle
of youth between duty and desire. (*He stares at the floor. She
regards him anxiously.*)

MRS. LIU. You seem the same — to me, Ming-kwan, and yet
you have changed. (*He looks up with a smile and a partial return of his former mood.*)

MING-KWAN. I am always the same — to you, honorable

mother. And yet it is true that I have changed, in many ways that you will discover after we have talked awhile. I have learned many subjects.

MRS. LIU. You are a student now, and your mother does not understand such things. But your father — (*She glances with evident disquiet toward L. She motions him to the empty chair.*) Come, let us talk. There is a little time — before your father returns.

MING-KWAN (*sitting*). Returns? Kong Su tells me that he is at home.

MRS. LIU. He is in his private room, conferring with Mr. King Chi-kwei.

MING-KWAN (*looking carelessly around the room*). Business — or a friendly chat?

MRS. LIU (*with a side glance at him*). A friendly chat — about business, I believe.

MING-KWAN (*crossing his legs and regarding her with a lazy smile*). And what business brings my father and Mr. King together? Father had better keep wide awake when he chats over the teacups with Mr. King Chi-kwei.

MRS. LIU (*watching him closely*). It may be that it has to do with you, Ming-kwan.

MING-KWAN (*suddenly alert*). With me? What concern regarding me would cause my father to call in the esteemed Mr. King?

MRS. LIU (*earnestly*). My son, whatever your father asks of you, please do it.

MING-KWAN. And what is my respected father going to ask of me?

MRS. LIU (*guardedly*). It may have to do with — with your new ideas.

MING-KWAN (*with a short laugh*). My new ideas? You mean that he will request me to give up my new ideas, as if ideas were like garments which one could put on and off at the will of — a parent? No, mother, ideas are not like that. They are not like clothes, to be shed at command. Rather, they are like the blood which courses through your veins. They are a part of you, your very living self. To renounce them, then, would be to renounce one's self. I am quite prepared to discuss this with my father.

MRS. LIU. But your father is angry, Ming-kwan, very angry with you, I fear. You must not oppose his wishes.

MING-KWAN. My father is unduly alarmed. I am not as unfilial as he evidently considers me. I have an open mind, I can be reasoned with. However, I flatter myself that I shall be able to win over my father to my way of thinking.

MRS. LIU. Then you do not know your father, Ming-kwan. *He* does not change. He is a man of iron will, and if he is opposed — (*She makes a little gesture.*)

MING-KWAN. I shall endeavor not to oppose him, but to reason with him. As soon as he has finished his business with Mr. King — (*pauses and frowns*). You say that his business has to do with me? If my father wishes to talk with me about my ideas, just why is he discussing it with Mr. King? I can't see any possible relation between my ideas and Mr. King Chi-kwei. (*He shakes his head in perplexity and studies the floor.*)

MRS. LIU (*with hesitation*). Ming-kwan.

MING-KWAN (*without looking up*). Yes, mother.

MRS. LIU. Why are you wearing a flower? I never knew you to do that before. (*He glances at the flower in the lapel of his coat and smiles at her.*)

MING-KWAN. A foreign custom — and a pretty one, I think. (*He touches the flower gently.*) It was given to me by a friend. (*A pause. He looks back at the floor with a shade of embarrassment.*)

MRS. LIU (*eyeing him*). I have heard that there are many young women at the college.

MING-KWAN. Yes, very many.

MRS. LIU. That is very strange. It would not have been allowed when I was a girl. (*A pause.*) Have you, by chance, looked upon any one of them with favor? (*He does not reply or look directly at her, but his hand goes up to caress the flower. She raises her eyebrows and nods knowingly.*) Then there is — someone?

MING-KWAN (*without looking up*). Yes, mother. (*She clenches her hands and glances out L. A pause.*)

MRS. LIU. It is all very irregular, my son. You have not consulted your father and your mother, and there has been no go-between.

MING-KWAN (*with sudden eagerness*). If you only knew her, mother, I'm sure you would be glad.

MRS. LIU (*forcing a smile*). Is she as radiant as a spring morning, and does her beauty rival the sun at midday? Is her cheek as delicate as the blush of the fairest flower and —

MING-KWAN (*echoing her banter*). And when she smiles, it is as though heaven had bestowed a gift of rarest jade — beautiful jade, mother. Her heart is as pure as a crystal fountain and her mind is —

MRS. LIU. Her *mind?* You consider *that?* (*She has unlocked his lips and he has now returned to his former insouciant gaiety.*)

MING-KWAN. Most certainly I do, since she is studying and making her living with her knowledge.

MRS. LIU. Her living? (*With a sigh*) Then her family — she works outside her home?

MING-KWAN. Horrible of crimes, my mother, she does. She is teaching to get money for her education.

MRS. LIU (*hesitatingly*). Do you — love her?

MING-KWAN. I surely do. (*In his quick embarrassment that causes him to look down, he does not notice her growing agitation.*)

MRS. LIU. And does she love — you?

MING-KWAN. She has not accepted me yet.

MRS. LIU. *Accepted* you? Must a young woman *accept* a

young man before they — they — Ming-kwan, I do not know
what to think. *I* did not accept your father. It was all arranged by my parents and the —

MING-KWAN (*nodding*). I know. The go-between. But we
are living in a new age, mother, an age of freedom. Young people today are learning to choose their mates for themselves, at
least (*he bows respectfully*) — without the *compulsion* of their
parents. For my part, I would never take a wife selected for
me through a go-between.

MRS. LIU (*alarmed*). Ming-kwan! You do not know what
you are saying. At first I thought that this might be a pretty
fancy of yours, but if you *mean* what you say, then — your
father — (*She checks herself and glances guiltily out L.*)

MING-KWAN. My *father!* What do you mean? (*He turns
quickly and looks out L., his face set and stern.*) Do I understand that my father is in there making arrangements for my
engagement? (*He faces her and speaks emphatically but with
respect*) When I marry, it will be the girl of my own choice, and
I shall be the man of *her* choice.

MRS. LIU (*rising in great agitation*). Ming-kwan, I did not
mean to say that — but — but if your father *does* ask you to
marry, you will not refuse, my son. Whatever your father requires of you will be, I fear — necessary.

MING-KWAN (*rising*). Necessary?

MRS. LIU. Do not be angry with me, Ming-kwan, for it is
your happiness, as well as our own, that I greatly desire.

MING-KWAN. For your happiness, mother, I would give up
almost anything except — except Lee Mei-york. (*He crosses
to L. She stares after him.*)

MRS. LIU (*softly*). So that is her name? (MING-KWAN *nods,
his gaze fixed out L.*) Mei-york — " beautiful jade." Now I
know why you said, " A gift of rarest jade." (*She approaches
him.*) Would she honor our ancestors?

MING-KWAN. She would honor them, of course, but she would

not worship them. (*With a gesture*) I cannot imagine her kow-towing to the moon or bowing down before Kwan Yin, the god-dess of mercy.

MRS. LIU (*clutching his arm*).   You are saying that — she is — (*she does not venture further*).

MING-KWAN (*quietly*).   Yes, she is a Christian.

MRS. LIU.   A *Christian?* My son, my son! If your father — you must not tell him. You do not understand. He would — (*The murmur of men's voices is heard outside L.*) Ming-kwan, he is coming! You will be wise! Promise me!

MING-KWAN.   I will be honest.

MRS. LIU (*in desperation*).   Do as your father desires, for we must — we *must* have the money.

MING-KWAN (*amazed*).   The money? What are you saying? Do you mean that my father has —

MRS. LIU (*stepping back*).   They are coming — Mr. King and your father. (*Enter* KING *and* MR. LIU *L*.   MR. LIU *glances quickly from* MING-KWAN *to* MRS. LIU *and back again at* MING-KWAN.)

MING-KWAN (*bowing*).   Father, I hope you are quite well.

MR. LIU.   I am quite well, Ming-kwan. I am glad to see you.

MING-KWAN (*bowing*).   I trust, Mr. King, that you are in excellent health.

KING.   Excellent, Ming-kwan. And you?

MING-KWAN.   I am quite well.

KING.   That is gratifying. You have impressed me as an ex-ceedingly sensible young man, Ming-kwan, and I predict great things for you. The business world has need of just such talents as you possess. I can congratulate you, Mr. Liu, on having such a son to honor the memory of your ancestors. (*Bows.*) And you, Mrs. Liu. (*She bows.*)

MR. LIU.   Convey our greetings to your august wife.

KING.   I shall be most happy. My wife and my daughter Chen-shu send their expressions of regard. They have spoken very graciously of you, Ming-kwan.

MING-KWAN (*with a stiff bow*).　Your august wife and your estimable daughter are most kind.

MR. LIU.　Our mutual friend, Mr. Weng Tai, will wait upon you shortly to negotiate our matter formally, Mr. King.

KING.　I shall receive him most gladly.

(*There are formal bows of farewell and they conduct* KING *to the door. As* MR. LIU *walks back toward the table, his back momentarily turned,* MRS. LIU *makes an appealing gesture to* MING-KWAN *and exits R.* MR. LIU *gives* MING-KWAN *an appraising glance. The atmosphere is tense. The attitude of the two men suggests the wariness of duelists awaiting the opening move of an opponent.* MR. LIU *is formal, precise, and self-contained, keeping his poise under stress of anger.* MING-KWAN, *except for a couple of flashes, is uniformly respectful, even when urging his opinions.*)

MING-KWAN.　I am here at your command, father.

MR. LIU (*sitting L. of the square table*).　It is well. There is much for us to discuss.

MING-KWAN (*with his arms straight by his side*).　I am all attention.

MR. LIU.　Be seated, Ming-kwan. (MING-KWAN *sits opposite his father.*) It is fitting for me to observe, my son, that when I allowed you to go to that college and agreed to pay your tuition and expenses, it was on the understanding that you would enter upon such studies as would best fit you to choose a profitable vocation. There are, I am sure, courses of study that would fit you to return to your home and take your place beside me in our business or accept some position in another firm at good pay. Or, perchance, in government employ.

MING-KWAN.　I have no desire to enter politics, and I am not inclined to a business career. I do not like bookkeeping and accounting and firm management and salesmanship and all that. I wish to devote my life to helping my fellow men.

MR. LIU (*with a lift of his eyebrows*).　Yes? And how?

MING-KWAN.　I wish to help China to realize the boundless

opportunities that open before her, opportunities which she can never grasp unless she introduces vast industrial reforms and trains herself in the social sciences.

MR. LIU (*in perplexity*). The social sciences?

MING-KWAN (*waxing enthusiastic*). Everything that has to do with the political, the industrial, the educational, the moral, and the spiritual welfare of society. (*He leans over the table.*) So I took up sociology, and I assure you, father, that it is indeed thrilling. I had not realized that our country had so much to learn before it could be reconstructed. Consider the subjects that I am studying — history of social thought and social ethics, industrial welfare, town and country community organizations, public health, criminology, penology, poverty and poor relief, social insurance, child welfare and —

MR. LIU (*lifting his hand*). That will do.

MING-KWAN. But I want you to understand what —

MR. LIU. I have heard all that is necessary. Will this jumble of subjects be of any use in advancing you in the world? Will they bring you in any money?

MING-KWAN. That is not causing me any concern. I am not preparing myself to make money.

MR. LIU (*tapping on the table*). Then might I inquire just what you *are* preparing yourself to do?

MING-KWAN. I wish to serve my country and my fellow men. I am particularly interested in industrial reform, because I clearly perceive that if our country does not organize its life aright, it will remain in bondage to its own ignorance and to other nations. Our people must be awakened to social injustice. Why, father, if you could see, as I have, the little boys and girls working in the dark, stuffy silk mills, match factories and cotton mills; children with swollen bodies and inflamed eyes and bowed shoulders and —

MR. LIU (*bringing his fist down on the table*). Enough of that. I have not asked you here to make speeches. It is very evident that you have disgraced yourself and your family by becoming a communist.

MING-KWAN. You are wrong, respected father. I am not a communist, although I do confess that there is much in their teaching to inspire one to noble, unselfish action. (MR. LIU *begins to tap impatiently on the table.*) No, China does not have to look outside for her salvation. (MRS. LIU *appears R. She stands just inside the door, unnoticed by the two men.*) Revolution? Yes, if we can achieve our ends in no other way, but I do not think that —

MR. LIU (*striking the table again*). Enough, I tell you. Revolution! So this is the result of my sending you to that college! You, my son, on whom I had relied to return here to assume your rightful family obligations and to be my other self in our family business. Revolution! Is this —

MING-KWAN (*desperately*). But you do not understand, honorable father. It is not that I —

MR. LIU. I understand all too well. You have made yourself abundantly clear. I have listened with patience, and beyond all reason, to what you have had to say. Doubtless the next thing that will assault my ears will be that you have become (*he leans forward and taps ominously on the table*) — a Christian! (MRS. LIU *gasps. There is a pause.* MING-KWAN *straightens and meets his father's gaze unflinchingly.*) You do not answer me! Is it true?

MING-KWAN (*quietly*). I do not know.

MR. LIU. What? You do not *know?* You mean, then, that you no longer believe in the faith and the honored customs of your ancestors? Is that so?

MING-KWAN. Yes, that is so. That there is truth in the great teachings, I admit; but I can no longer believe in the superstitions. I do not believe in evil spirits, in ancestor worship, in kneeling down, in burning incense and red paper, and in —

MRS. LIU (*clasping her hands in agony*). Ming-kwan, my son, my son! (MING-KWAN *rises quickly and turns toward her. His face softens, and he makes as though to hold out his arms to her, but checks himself and turns again to his father, who has arisen and is standing, stern and erect, by the table.*)

MR. LIU.   Have you anything else — to say?

MING-KWAN (*with a bow*).   Only this, honorable father. You accuse me of being a communist and you ask me if I am a Christian. I can but reply that I am a seeker after the truth.

MR. LIU (*scornfully*).   The truth! (*Waxing angry*) What can you, an upstart of a youth, know about — (*He checks himself and, turning to the table, picks up the newspaper clipping. With a manifest effort at self-control and dignity, he plays for time by pretending to scan the clipping, frowning as he does so. Then, with icy politeness, he holds out the clipping to* MING-KWAN.) You admit that you are the writer? (MING-KWAN *nods respectfully.*) And you continue to believe in its worthless sentiments?

MING-KWAN.   My self-respect forbids me to deny it.

MR. LIU (*with sudden scorn*).   Your self-respect! If you had a shred of self-respect, you would at once acknowledge that you had forfeited all right to be considered —

MRS. LIU.   Wen-chin! You cannot!

MING-KWAN.   Mother, my father is quite right (*he bows deferentially*) — from his own standpoint.

(*A pause while* MR. LIU *regards his son through slightly narrowed eyelids, as if measuring the full meaning of this last remark. He places the clipping back on the table and walks slowly L., tapping his clenched right hand into the palm of the left hand. Then he turns and addresses* MING-KWAN *with studied dignity.*)

MR. LIU.   I have heard many words today regarding the nation and society and reforms and other interesting matters, but I have yet to hear you mention your obligation to — your family. Am I to understand that you still regard yourself as a filial son?

MING-KWAN.   Most certainly, father, within the limits of my conscience.

MR. LIU.   We shall not inquire into that at this moment. It is sufficient for our present purpose that you continue to admit your relationship to your father and to your mother and to this home which is the center of our family and which possesses the proud leadership of our clan.

MING-KWAN. I could not wish to deny it.

MR. LIU. Allow me to admonish you that there is no higher duty than that which requires of a son that he subordinate his own interests, even his own happiness, to the higher claims that his family have upon his life. That much, I am sure, you have not forgotten while at the college.

MING-KWAN (*with a bow*). I have not forgotten.

MR. LIU (*sits L.*). That is well. You are now in your home and able to view your circumstances with calm wisdom and under the guidance of your father's mature experience.

MING-KWAN. But, honorable father, I cannot deny what I —

MR. LIU (*raising his hand*). I have listened to you. Now you, my son, will listen to me. Before I inform you of my decision regarding your future, I shall briefly state the regrettable financial circumstances in which I find myself involved. I am sorry to tell you that the trade in dried fruits is in lamentable condition. It is absolutely necessary that I have some financial assistance. (*He looks at the floor and shakes his head slowly.* MING-KWAN *glances at his mother.*)

MING-KWAN. I am indeed distressed to learn of this.

MR. LIU (*looking up*). Your expression of feeling is gratifying. But a way has been provided. Our friend, the excellent Mr. King Chi-kwei, will supply me with the necessary money. Such generosity on his part merits our highest appreciation. (MING-KWAN *is staring at his father, alert and watchful, as if sensing what is to follow.*)

MING-KWAN. We cannot but be grateful to Mr. King.

MR. LIU. Our gratitude will be measured by deeds, not words. I shall expect you to recognize this.

MING-KWAN. In what way, father?

MR. LIU. First of all, you will give up your present foolish studies and take some courses that will fit you to return within a short time and take your place by my side in our dry fruit business.

MING-KWAN. Give up — my sociology?

MR. LIU. By your own confession the subjects that now engage your attention will not train you for a business career.

MING-KWAN. I am not adapted to a business career. My inclinations and abilities lie along other lines. I do not wish, father, to refuse you my help in this emergency, but —

MR. LIU (*with growing sternness*). My judgment is superior to yours. May I add that Mr. King thinks highly of your commercial possibilities and thus endorses my opinion.

MING-KWAN. Does Mr. King make this one of the conditions of the loan?

MR. LIU (*somewhat nonplussed by this unexpected frontal attack*). I — I did not so state the matter, my son, but it is altogether possible that he does regard it in such a light.

MING-KWAN. Please speak frankly, father. What relation is there between my vocation — and the loan? (MR. LIU *pauses and measures* MING-KWAN *keenly.*)

MR. LIU. Mr. King has a natural and very understandable interest in the career of his future son-in-law. (MRS. LIU *is gazing apprehensively at her son, who has suddenly stiffened. A quick spasm of pain contorts his features. He then reasserts his self-control and his face becomes as grave and as impassive as his father's.*)

MING-KWAN. Did I hear you aright, honorable father? Did you say — son-in-law?

MR. LIU. Your mother and I have conferred upon the matter and it is our wish that you marry King Chen-shu. I have had conversations with Mr. King and I find that he and his wife agree that an alliance between our families is most desirable. (MING-KWAN *looks at his mother, who finds it hard to meet his questioning gaze.*)

MING-KWAN (*with a bitter smile*). The old dragon of ancient custom may be dying, but he can still thrash about with his tail.

MR. LIU (*frowning*). I do not follow you, my son.

MING-KWAN. No, most honorable father, you would not. (*Slowly*) You are giving me to understand that Mr. King, as a condition of his lending you this money — a condition not directly stated, perhaps, but implied in true Chinese fashion — that as a condition of your receiving this money I am to give up my studies in sociology, take a business course, and return here to marry Chen-shu and settle down in business with you? (MR. LIU *does not reply, but a half-unconscious nodding of his head gives* MING-KWAN *his answer.*) In plain language, you are selling me to Mr. King in return for his money. (MRS. LIU *gives a gasp and* MR. LIU *grips the edge of the tea table to control his anger.*)

MR. LIU. I do not deign to notice the unhappy manner in which you express yourself.

MING-KWAN. I regret, honorable father, if my language seems rather blunt, but I can see no advantage in evading the issue. (*A pause.*) And what if it does not seem possible for me to accept?

MR. LIU (*grimly*). That, my son, would be most unfortunate, if you still wish to regard yourself (*with emphasis*) as my son. I entertain the hope that you will not refuse your filial responsibility.

MING-KWAN. I have no wish to disregard my filial responsibility, but there still remains the fact that I may interpret my duty to my family somewhat differently.

MR. LIU. I trust that this may not be the case. It is my desire to give you the customary time for reflection, if the matter seems doubtful to you, but unfortunately it is necessary for me to complete certain business arrangements as soon as possible.

MING-KWAN. I do not need time for reflection. My duty is clear to me. I have my answer ready.

MR. LIU (*leaning forward*). And that answer — is? (MRS. LIU *bends forward, staring at* MING-KWAN. *Mr. Liu's face is impassive.*)

MING-KWAN (*looking from one to the other*).   It is with great
regret that my answer must be — no!   (MRS. LIU *gives a little
cry*.   MR. LIU *rises slowly, his eyes burning into Ming-kwan's*.)

MR. LIU.   Do you wish to give me any reason for this — this
unfilial, outrageous conduct?

MING-KWAN.   I do.   Much as I respect you and my honored
mother, I do not consider that I am to be traded about like so
much property.   I do not wish to marry King Chen-shu because
(*he straightens up*) — I am in love with another girl.

MR. LIU (*coldly*).   And who is this girl who has enticed you
into this ridiculous infatuation?

MING-KWAN (*with heat*).   She has not enticed me.   She is too
fine, too upright, too high-minded for that.   (*He has himself in
leash again*.)   As a matter of fact, she has, so far, refused to
accept me.   Her name is Lee Mei-york, and she is the daughter
of a farmer in Foochow.

MR. LIU.   So!   This strumpet of a farmer's daughter — a
farmer's daughter — has —   (MING-KWAN *flares and takes a
quick step forward*.)

MING-KWAN.   Father!   You cannot — (*he relaxes and bows*).
Your pardon, honorable father, but you do not understand that
Lee Mei-york is an intelligent, cultured student at college, and
more than worthy of the position of daughter-in-law in your
home.

MR. LIU.   The daughter of a *farmer!*   Is she, in addition, a
Christian?

MING-KWAN.   She is, honorable father.   (MR. LIU *sits again
at the tea table and points his finger at* MING-KWAN.)

MR. LIU.   It is she, then, who has led you away from the faith
of your ancestors?

MING-KWAN.   I freely confess that it is her beautiful life that
has influenced me greatly.   But there are other influences —
the teachings, the life of Jesus Christ, and the life of my professor of sociology, Dr. Cochran.   Mei-york wishes me to become
a Christian but she insists that I do not do so unless my mind is
fully persuaded.   She will not have me confess the faith simply

for her sake. I do wish to believe — in something; for I am persuaded that China can be truly helped only by believing sons. (MR. LIU, *who has been following* MING-KWAN *intently, now shrugs his shoulders.*)

MR. LIU. As for that, you may think in your mind what you wish. I only require that on your return here you will faithfully perform the ritual duties that will devolve upon you as a member of our honored family. (*A slight pause.* MING-KWAN *regards his father steadily.*)

MING-KWAN. I cannot do with my body what my soul abhors as untrue.

MR. LIU. The time for discussion and argument is past. Once again I ask you — will you obey our wishes?

MRS. LIU (*laying her hand pleadingly on Ming-kwan's arm*). My son, do as your father asks, or we shall all be ruined.

MING-KWAN (*starting violently*). Ruined? You mean — that unless I give my consent Mr. King will not lend the money and that this will result in financial disaster for my father?

MRS. LIU. Yes, Ming-kwan, that is so.

MING-KWAN. My father! (MING-KWAN *looks imploringly at* MR. LIU, *who slightly inclines his head.*)

MR. LIU. It is true.

MING-KWAN. But surely there is another way. Cannot the money be secured from someone else?

MRS. LIU. Do you desire to see your father in the clutches of the professional money lenders? (*A silence.* MING-KWAN *presses his hands together and stares at the floor. His parents watch him intently. He raises his head, takes a deep breath, and spreads out his hands.*)

MING-KWAN. Father, rather than have you face such a disaster, I will, for the present, forsake my career and come back to help you in your business.

MR. LIU. You will, then, do *all* that I ask?

MING-KWAN (*clenching his hands*). Honorable father!

MR. LIU. Your untrained services could not avert the catastrophe. There must be — money.

MRS. LIU. Ming-kwan, obey your father. Be a filial son.

MING-KWAN. Obey! Filial! (*In an agony of indecision he walks R. and stands with folded arms, his head bent in thought. MRS. LIU comes over beside MR. LIU and they engage in a brief conversation. She sits beside the tea table and pleads with him. He shakes his head from time to time. With a shrug of his shoulders and a gesture of finality he rises and walks toward the long table. MRS. LIU rises also and stands, wide-eyed and fearful, staring at MING-KWAN. MR. LIU, his back to MING-KWAN, studies the scrolls on the rear wall with elaborate effort to seem casual. MING-KWAN looks at him. A wan smile edges Ming-kwan's lips, and he shakes his head sadly. As MR. LIU turns, he notes that MING-KWAN is watching him. MR. LIU folds his arms across his breast and raises his eyebrows in silent inquiry.*)

MING-KWAN. Honorable father.

MR. LIU. I trust that you have considered — well and carefully. (MING-KWAN *takes a few steps forward and drops his arms to his side. He bows deferentially. Then, raising his head, looks his father squarely in the face.*)

MING-KWAN. I have considered — well and carefully.

MR. LIU (*impassively*). Your answer, my son.

MING-KWAN. I am quite willing to forsake, for the time being, my own ambitions — no, they are more than ambitions, they are dreams. I am willing to return and help you in the business, but I am not willing to observe the ancient customs of worship and I will not marry King Chen-shu. (*Almost fiercely*) You have not the right, honorable father, to force me by your necessity. (MRS. LIU *clasps her hands and bows her head. A quiver runs through Mr. Liu's body and his hands tighten on his biceps. His eyes narrow slightly but his face remains impassive.*)

MR. LIU. Your decision is — final?

MING-KWAN. My decision is final.

MR. LIU. No matter what the consequences?

MING-KWAN (*with a break in his voice*). No matter what the consequences.

Mr. Liu (*with flat-toned coldness*).   Very well, my son — that *was*.   (Mrs. Liu *raises her head and shivers apprehensively.*) You are untrue to every consideration of filial piety and the consequences must be suffered (*he glances at* Mrs. Liu *and his voice wavers*) by all of us.   (*A pause.* Ming-kwan *clenches his hands.* Mr. Liu, *once again stern and unyielding, regards his son from head to foot.*)   Either you will consent to all of my commands, *all* of them, or not one cash will you receive from me for your education and your living.   Moreover, I will erase your name from the family (Ming-kwan *bows his head and closes his eyes*) and after seven days I will proclaim to all the world that henceforth you are no longer my son.

Mrs. Liu (*in agony*).   Wen-chin! Our son, our son!

Ming-kwan (*brokenly*).   My father!

(*A pause. Ming-kwan's head is still bowed.* Mr. Liu *is gazing at him with cold, unemotional sternness. As* Ming-kwan *raises his head and meets his father's eyes,* Mr. Liu *drops his arms to his side.*)

Mr. Liu.   For the last time — will you obey?

(Ming-kwan *looks at his mother. Her utter despair grips him and he takes a step forward, with half-raised arms. She responds with an eloquent gesture of appeal. Ming-kwan's shoulders sag a trifle and he closes his eyes once more. Then they flash open and he stretches out his arms to* Mr. Liu.)

Ming-kwan.   I cannot, honorable father. Before God — I *cannot*.

(Mr. Liu *flings out his arms and points, in final dismissal, out R.* Ming-kwan, *with one last look at his mother, bows and exits slowly with bent head, R. A sob breaks from Mrs. Liu's lips and she buries her face in her hands.* Mr. Liu, *with immobile face, folds his arms and gazes, unseeing, straight ahead. When he finally speaks it is with richness of tone and with the awe of unanswered question.*)

Mr. Liu (*slowly*).   Before — God!

CURTAIN

THE LORD'S PRAYER*

by

François Coppée

CHARACTERS

MADEMOISELLE ROSE
ZÉLEE, *her housekeeper*
MÈRE BLANCHE, *a neighbor*
THE CURÉ
JACQUES LE ROUX
AN OFFICER
SOLDIERS

Scene: A living room in a home in Paris.
Time: During the French Commune.

THE LORD'S PRAYER*

A room on the ground floor with a door and two windows, looking out over a small sunlit garden full of rosebushes in flower. Through the open gate and beyond the garden, which is enclosed by a low wall, is seen a suburban lane; and in the distance, high factory chimneys. The furniture of the room is simple; a plain sideboard, a round table, some chairs, a wicker armchair. At left, a fireplace. On the mantel, a colored plaster statue of the Virgin. At right, a roll-top desk, and a mahogany bookcase filled with books. On the walls, a large ivory crucifix and two religious pictures. Doors at right and left.

When the curtain rises, ZÉLEE, *an old woman in peasant's dress and cap, is seated in an alert attitude. Standing near her is* MÈRE BLANCHE, *a woman of the Paris environs. She is hatless and carries a basket of provisions on her arm.*

MÈRE BLANCHE.   You are sure? He is really killed? (ZÉLEE *nods.*) There must be some mistake. It's too terrible!

ZÉLEE.   There can't be any. Listen! It was near here — in Rue Haxe — yesterday afternoon. The rebels were carrying everything before them. The abbé was against the wall with the others — he was speaking — he raised his hand to *bless* them — and then — then — he fell — shot dead. When they took him as a hostage four days ago, Mademoiselle Rose had no fear. " We shall have him back again soon," she said. He was so good, so beloved! Oh, the brutes, to shoot him down! (*Sound as of volley of shots is heard in the distance.*)

MÈRE BLANCHE.   What is that?

ZÉLEE (*starting up*).   The soldiers from Versailles! That

* A new translation by Mary Aldis.

197

is right. Kill the rebels! Butcher them! It will serve them right!

MÈRE BLANCHE. Hush! You don't know what you're saying! Last night the brook ran red with blood. More than one innocent man was killed.

ZÉLEE. And who more innocent than my poor master — so strong, so tender, a true father to his people — keeping nothing for himself, giving away all that he had! — To kill him! — When your passions are aroused, you Parisians are like wild beasts! It's "For the Commune," is it? It's the lust to kill!

MÈRE BLANCHE. Where is Mademoiselle Rose? She worshiped her brother.

ZÉLEE. At first she did not say a word. I was frightened. I thought she was going mad, and then — she cried out against Paris. "The horror, the horror!" At last, she dropped off to sleep in his armchair. (*Points toward R.*) Just now in her sleep, I heard her grind her teeth.

MÈRE BLANCHE. Poor girl!

ZÉLEE. I came to them fifteen years ago. The abbé was a boy of ten and Mademoiselle Rose only eighteen — so pretty, so young, so tender of little Jean! Their father and mother were dead — they were alone — the two young things. He was always reading. She was so proud when he brought home prizes from school. Then he went away to the seminary. We were so lonely! A rich farmer wanted to marry her, but she said she must take care of little Jean. "When he is a priest," she said, "I will keep his house." And she kept her word. And now he is dead and she is alone! (*She bursts into sobs. The voice of Mademoiselle Rose comes from the room beyond.*)

MADEMOISELLE ROSE. Zélee!

ZÉLEE. She is awake. You had better go. She must not talk.

MÈRE BLANCHE. Of course. Good night. God keep you. (*Exits at back.*)

(*After a moment enter* MADEMOISELLE ROSE *from R., un-*

steadily. ZÉLEE *goes to her tenderly and supports her to a chair.*)

ZÉLEE. You are better? Have you slept?

MADEMOISELLE ROSE. Yes — but the dreams! The row of prisoners against the wall, the crack of the guns — they fall quickly, one after another. I can't blot it out. (ZÉLEE *brings water which she drinks eagerly.*) I heard the guns in my sleep. Are they fighting still?

ZÉLEE. No, they say the last rebels were captured at Père la Chaise.

MADEMOISELLE ROSE (*pointing to the garden*). See how the roses drop their petals. Look at the sunshine on the grass; the birds are singing. And my brother, my brother is dead! (*She rocks herself to and fro.*) How did you know the rebels were taken?

ZÉLEE. Mère Blanche told me. She has just gone.

MADEMOISELLE ROSE. The woman who lives at the end of the street? My brother was good to her.

ZÉLEE. Monsieur le Curé has been here. I said you were asleep. He promised to return.

MADEMOISELLE ROSE. I can't see him.

ZÉLEE. Mademoiselle! Think again. He loved Abbé Jean. They were friends. It is his right to come.

MADEMOISELLE ROSE. Oh, well, let him come; but if he dares try to comfort me, if he talks about resignation, I can't bear it. I won't be told about the justice and goodness of God! I won't! Zélee, I shall live for a long, long time. I am very strong. The days and the weeks and the years will follow each other. The little clock there will keep on ticking them off, one after another, over and over and over, until I am an old woman. And always I'll be here. Animals that are no longer of use they kill. What am I to do now? They have taken away from me my child, my little brother. I am no longer of use. What can be done with me? If I could avenge his death, bring his murderers to justice! But I am helpless! And God lets such things be! I tell you, if

God exists, he is false or he is powerless. He lets an innocent man die so! I was a fool to believe in him, in his goodness, his mercy. Let them not talk to me of heaven — there is no God! (*While she has been speaking the* CURÉ, *an old white-haired priest, has come in. He stops at the threshold of the open door, not hearing Mademoiselle Rose's last words. She turns quickly.*)

ZÉLEE.   It is the curé. (*She goes out. The* CURÉ *comes toward* MADEMOISELLE ROSE.)

CURÉ.   My poor child, my poor, poor child!

MADEMOISELLE ROSE.   Thank you for coming, Monsieur le Curé; but can we not talk — a little later? You loved him, I know. I do not wish to be unkind — only I can't speak of it. I can't! Leave me alone, I beg of you.

CURÉ.   If I am unwelcome, I will go, but — a holy priest of God has submitted to martyrdom. I wish to say to you one word. Be comforted — your brother is with the saints of God. He is in heaven.

MADEMOISELLE ROSE.   Ah, I was waiting for that! You say my brother is in heaven! I say he is in the Rue Haxe, bloody, horrible, pierced with gunshots — that I can see. I cannot see him in heaven with a palm in his hand among your saints! I tell you those ghouls who killed him, who threw his body into a pit and covered him with clay and stones, destroyed my faith in heaven. Do you understand now? I suppose you think it is shining, your heaven, calm and blue and serene, while Paris is burning, while the pavements are red and slippery with blood. Sodom and Gomorrah are come again. But he was good, my brother. What has he done that he should be part of that? Your heaven, I don't believe in it! I defy God! I have said it. Curse me if you will.

CURÉ.   My child, I weep for you. What you say does not frighten me. God will forgive you when you ask his forgiveness — as you will ask it; but in the holiness with which he has been invested, in his glory among the angels, your brother's heart is rent by the blasphemies of his unhappy sister.

MADEMOISELLE ROSE. Oh, forgive me! I am beside myself. But if he is in paradise, as you say, how can I live on here? When he was little, I cared for him; when he became a priest, noble and strong, I looked up to him as to a father. I served him — I took care of him — he took no thought for himself. Every evening he would read — here — by this lamp — and I would sew near him. Often we would both speak at the same moment of the same thing, so close were our thoughts. For his sake I refused to marry. When he was absent I stitched my thoughts of him into the garments I made for him; and I was happy. I owe him everything, and now! My grief is precious to me — a cruel joy. My last breath will be to mourn for him — my brother.

CURÉ. Poor, broken heart! Your tears will water a green spot in the desert of your empty future. My child, guard your suffering in your heart, but keep always in your mind the knowledge that he knows all you think, all you do. I speak now not as the curé, but as an old man who has seen life and loves you. I feel the spirit of your brother hovering near us. It is as if he said: "Weep if you must, my sister, your tears are dear to me; but weep with courage. Hold ever in your heart the memory of former days, and the hope of those to come. Live nobly. I will watch over you. Read aloud the Holy Book, and as you hear the divine words you will think that you hear the echo of my voice. When you succor those unfortunate ones whom I have loved, you will feel the pressure of my hand in their handclasp. Travel, then, the length of the way marked out for you. I, your invisible guide, will help you bear your burden of sorrow. Be not troubled that the hour is afar off when the blessed dawn of your immortal day shall break in holy light upon your vision. Be patient to the end."

MADEMOISELLE ROSE. Oh, Monsieur le Curé, if it were true! But it is not true! Oh, why cannot I die too? (*Firing is heard again in the distance.*)

CURÉ. They are still fighting.

MADEMOISELLE ROSE. What's that? Oh, yes, I remember, the Commune is beaten. The rebels are killed. (*With a hoarse triumphant cry*) My brother is avenged!

CURÉ. Who knows who is killed? There may be many who are innocent.

MADEMOISELLE ROSE. How can you pity them? They are murderers! (*More shots are heard.*) Do you hear that? The sound of the guns makes me glad. I am mad for vengeance! If they need anyone to excite the soldiers, to shoot down the rebels, let them come to me; I am ready!

CURÉ. And it is his sister who says this!

MADEMOISELLE ROSE. Can't you understand? My brother — my brother was killed! Do you hear? Shot down after all the years of patient devoted self-sacrifice! The moment their passions are aroused, they shoot him down. Have they souls? Look! (*She opens a cupboard and takes out a black cassock and a priest's round hat.*) See how worn and shabby these are. I hid them so that he might get new ones. But when I told him, he looked at me with his tender smile. "Rose," he said, "I have just been to see the Duvals. There are five mouths to feed now, and another coming. Sister Rose, please give me back my old clothes. You will mend them?" And four days later he was in prison as a hostage, and there was no one to pay his ransom! And you stand there and bid me remember to pardon! You try to rock my bitterness to sleep with your pity — but the sound of those muskets firing upon traitors calls to me. I glory in their punishment!

CURÉ (*sternly*). If I thought but of the dignity due the office I hold, I should pass the threshold of that door and never return. I should pronounce denunciation upon a rebellious soul and go away. But the God whom you defy is the same God your brother worshiped. I dare to affirm that at the moment of his death your brother raised his hand in blessing and in supplication for pardon: "Father, forgive them, they know not what they do." Hate, curse, denounce, if you must, unhappy woman that you are. But remember that if your brother could speak to those who caused his death, it would be in pity for their blindness and in forgiveness for their cruelty. (*Goes toward the door.*) Good-by.

MADEMOISELLE ROSE. My brother was a saint, and I am but a woman. What is to become of me? What shall I do?

CURÉ. Pray. (*Exits slowly, leaving the door open.*)

MADEMOISELLE ROSE (*alone*). He said to pray. My heart is full of hatred. I can never pray again. (*She takes her rosary and after a moment begins haltingly*) Our Father, who art in heaven, hallowed be thy name. Thy kingdom come, thy — thy — will — be done — Oh, I can't! — Give us this day our daily bread, and forgive us our trespasses (*pause*) — as we forgive those who trespass against us — forgive! forgive whom? Those murderers? No! I will *never* forgive them — by the beads of this rosary — (*She gazes at the rosary, then throws it upon the table.*) He said my brother forgave them. I will never, never forgive them! (*At this moment a bareheaded, disheveled man wearing the uniform of a Communist enters quickly at the back by the gate into the garden. Before closing the gate, he looks quickly in either direction, then rapidly crosses the little garden and comes into the room, shutting the door behind him.*)

JACQUES LE ROUX. At last, shelter! (MADEMOISELLE ROSE *gives a cry of anger and surprise.*) For the love of God, let me stay!

MADEMOISELLE ROSE. A rebel, in my house!

LE ROUX. I am a fugitive. They are tracking me to my death as they track a hunted animal. If they take me they will shoot me against the wall. I saw your garden gate. You will hide me? Give me a corner where I can lie hid for one day, only one. I promise to go tomorrow. Turn me out now, and I am lost. You love some man — father, son, husband, brother! I implore you, save my life in the name of the man you love!

MADEMOISELLE ROSE (*slowly*). You ask that I save you " in the name of the man I love." Know, then, I had a brother whom

I loved. He was shot yesterday, against a wall — the Abbé Morel!

LE ROUX. I am lost. Let me go!

MADEMOISELLE ROSE. You have said it. Lost! Yes, go forth and I will go too. I will follow you to the street and I will cry to the crowd, "There is the assassin!"

LE ROUX. I am no assassin. I fought as others fought. I am innocent of crime. Have mercy!

MADEMOISELLE ROSE. You are all murderers. How dare you ask for mercy? (*She takes up the cassock.*) Look at this coat my brother wore because he gave away all his money to you — you, his murderers! And you pray to me for mercy!

LE ROUX. I see I cannot touch you. You are too cruel. Since you rejoice that I am to die, I will tell you who I am. Jacques Le Roux, member of the Commune.

MADEMOISELLE ROSE. You!

LE ROUX. I voted against the revolution. I opposed the shooting of hostages. Still, I have fought against the government. I am not a believer, yet I reverence and trust those who worship God. Now I find what the goodness of a Christian woman means. You have no pity, you have no heart. How dare you pretend to worship the memory of Christ, you who will not forgive a man who is innocent — you, who will deliver up to his death a hunted fugitive who begs you for an asylum!

ZÉLEE (*enters quickly*). Mademoiselle Rose! Mademoiselle Rose! Soldiers are here to search the house. (*She sees* LE ROUX *and stifles a cry of surprise.*)

MADEMOISELLE ROSE. Tell them I will come. Go. (*Exit* ZÉLEE.) — He said my brother forgave all!

LE ROUX (*looking at her*). There is nothing for it, then, but death. Well, if it's my fate — (*She takes the cassock and hat from the chair and holds them out to* LE ROUX. *With the other hand she opens a door at the R., motioning him to a room within.*)

MADEMOISELLE ROSE. Go in there. Put them on. (*A sound

of loud knocking is heard at the gate.) Go quickly! (*She makes an imperious gesture, and* LE ROUX *takes the garments from her and obeys.* MADEMOISELLE ROSE *closes the door and stands by it.*) Have I done as you would wish, my brother? Oh, my beloved, my beloved! Give me some sign that I have done your will! (*An* OFFICER, *followed by several soldiers, enters.*)

OFFICER. Madam, your pardon! One of the rebels is concealed somewhere in this street — a leader — we must find him. Will you answer my questions or shall we search the house? It will go hard with you if he is found here.

MADEMOISELLE ROSE. Certainly I will answer your questions. There is no one here. Look if you choose. (*The* OFFICER *glances about, sees the image of the Virgin, and the pictures, and steps back embarrassed.*) Do you wish proofs? Indeed, I have no sympathy with rebels. (*At this moment* LE ROUX *in cassock and hat appears at the door R., stopping as if in amazement as he perceives the soldiers.*) I live here alone with my brother — ah, here he is. (OFFICER *respectfully touches his cap to the supposed priest.*)

OFFICER. Pardon, Monsieur l'Abbé! Monsieur — Madam. (*To his soldiers*) March! (*Exit, back, followed by soldiers.*)

LE ROUX (*extending his hand to* MADEMOISELLE ROSE). My children! My wife!

MADEMOISELLE ROSE (*holding up her hand to silence him*). It was for him, my brother. You wear his cassock. You are safe. Go. (*She points toward the door.* LE ROUX, *uncovering his head, goes slowly out.* MADEMOISELLE ROSE, *when alone, takes up the rosary from the table, pressing it to her lips, then falls upon her knees.*) Forgive us our trespasses as we forgive those who trespass against us.

CURTAIN

TWENTIETH CENTURY LULLABY*

by

Cedric Mount

CHARACTERS

MARY SMITH
THE SCHOOLMASTER
THE CLERGYMAN
THE ANNOUNCER
THE BUSINESSMAN
THE BRIDE
THE POLITICIAN
THE MADONNA

Scene: A nursery in England.
Time: Any evening, the present.

TWENTIETH CENTURY LULLABY

MARY SMITH *is sitting by the fireside in the nursery, gently rocking to and fro the cradle in which her baby is lying. As she rocks, she sings a lullaby. The lamps have not been lit and the only light comes from the fire, which throws a warm glow on* MARY *and the cradle, and casts strange leaping shadows over the rest of the room.*

MARY (*singing*).
> Hush-a-bye, baby, on the tree top,
> When the wind blows, the cradle will rock.
> When the bough breaks, the cradle will fall;
> Down will come baby, cradle and all.

(*She peeps at the baby for a moment, and then goes on singing, more softly.*)
> Hush-a-bye, baby, on the tree top,
> When the wind blows, the cradle will rock.
> When the bough —

(*She peeps again, and, satisfied that the baby is asleep, stops singing. But she does not take her eyes off the child, nor get up from her stool by the cradle. And presently she begins to talk to the sleeping infant, as mothers will.*)

MARY. There's my precious! (*She tucks him in.*) Sleep well! And soon you'll grow up into a fine big boy, won't you, my darling? And everyone will say, "Look at Peter Ulric Smith — isn't he the bonniest boy you ever saw?" And then you'll go to school and the master will teach you all sorts of clever things. And you'll learn them all so quickly! "Peter Ulric Smith," he'll say, "you've got a brain in a million. If all my pupils were as easy to teach as you are, my job would be a pleasure," he'll say —

209

(At this moment another voice — a man's — starts speaking from the other side of the room, and in a patch of light among the shadows we see the SCHOOLMASTER *standing, dressed in mortarboard and black gown. He seems to be talking to someone we cannot see, and* MARY *takes not the slightest notice of him, but goes on whispering to her baby. The only difference is that now we cannot hear her because of the Schoolmaster's loud and rather sarcastic voice.)*

SCHOOLMASTER. Peter Ulric Smith! There's a name to give a boy! Did you ever hear anything like it? *(He pauses for a second, with a rather sneering smile on his face, and in that second we hear* MARY *saying to the baby —)*

MARY. It's a very nice name, really — but you needn't tell the other boys what the " U " stands for if you don't want them to know.

SCHOOLMASTER. I could forgive the name if you had brains, but really you seem to be even more woolly-witted than most boys of your age — and that's saying a great deal. God knows why I spend my life teaching you and a hundred other brats like you, when I might have been doing something really useful — sweeping the streets or mining coal, for instance. How I'm going to cram enough knowledge into your brain-box to get you through your beastly little examinations I can't imagine —

MARY *(still talking to her baby)*. And my clever son's going to pass all his examinations — right at the top of the list — isn't he? Eh?

SCHOOLMASTER. Still, don't let us exaggerate the importance of examinations. The most important thing you've got to learn, Peter *Ulric* Smith, is that learning doesn't really matter a damn. Any cad can learn the sort of thing you find in books. What we want is a race of young men who can play games for the honor of the old school — and cheat and lie a little when called upon to do so.

MARY. Of course I want you to take an interest in sport, too, but you will remember that lessons are more important, won't you, my precious? And do be careful not to hurt yourself playing any nasty rough games —

schoolmaster. Those are the most important things, of course, but I expect your beastly parents will fret if I don't teach you a whole lot of unnecessary things into the bargain, so you'd better learn a spot of Latin as well. Eh? I'm damned if I really know why — except that we always have taught a spot of Latin. And anyway, we've got all the textbooks now, and we can't waste 'em.

mary. And then you must learn French — and German — and Spanish. Then when you grow up you can be a diplomat, or an ambassador, or something important like that —

schoolmaster. Who wants to learn French and German? Now you listen to me! My father went round the world three times — and he never knew a word of French and German — nor Spanish for that matter. "If English is good enough for me," he used to say, "it's good enough for these damned foreigners. Why should I take the trouble to learn their damned language? It'd only give them an exaggerated idea of their importance." That's what he used to say — and he was right! Now then — *amo, amas, amat* —

mary. Or perhaps you'd rather go into the church? That would be nice, too. Then I could go to service and listen to you preaching. You know, Peter, I think I'd like that best of all. And then you could christen all the little babies — just like that nice clergyman with the white hair christened you —

(*As* mary *goes on talking to her baby, we see the nice* clergy-man *with the white hair. He is standing at the other side of the room, quite near the* schoolmaster, *and his face is lit up by the dancing light from the fireplace, as he intones —*)

clergyman. I baptize you Peter Ulric, in the name of the Father, and of the Son, and of the Holy Ghost. (*He makes a gesture with his hand as though baptizing an invisible baby.*)

MARY. That would be nice, but I won't influence you or persuade you — I promise I won't. My baby shall choose just what he wants to do for himself, shan't he, my precious?

(*As* MARY *says this, another man's voice — a caressing, musical, condescending voice — begins to speak from the shadows, and then a flicker of light shows us that it is an* ANNOUNCER *in evening dress, speaking into a microphone.*)

ANNOUNCER. Juvenile unemployment, says the Savant Committee report, issued today, has reached so serious a pitch that vocational training and selection can no longer safely be left to the individual or the parent. The committee recommends that a board of psychoanalysts and efficiency experts be set up to examine all children of pre-employable age and determine on the career for which they are best fitted. The report further suggests that the surplus or nonemployable juvenile population be drafted into government instructional centers, to be trained in the art of employing enforced leisure. . . .

MARY. Of course, they do say it's hard for boys to get jobs nowadays when they leave school — but it won't be hard for my Ulric, will it, my sweet? You'll always be able to find a nice job —

ANNOUNCER. Here are the latest unemployment figures. The total number of persons unemployed at twelve noon today was three millions, four hundred and twenty-seven thousand, six hundred and one, an increase of one on the previous day's figures.

MARY. And oh, my darling, when you do grow up and go out into the world, there are two things I want you always to remember —

CLERGYMAN. Put your trust in God, and love thy neighbor as thyself —

SCHOOLMASTER. Never take anything or anybody on trust. Look after Number One and do the other fellow down if necessary —

MARY. And whatever you do, always be honest and honorable — and never tell a lie —

(*On these words we hear another voice, a thick, rasping, bullying voice. And then we see the* BUSINESSMAN *to whom it belongs — a plump, florid creature, flashily dressed and smoking a fat cigar.*)

BUSINESSMAN. Now look here, Smith, you've been with us for over a year, and I don't deny you've done pretty well. You're intelligent and you've got a certain talent for organization, but that's not enough. I'm not in business for my health, and I want someone who can show results. Now, take our advertising. It's all right — artistic and all that — but it's got no punch. And it don't make our products look worth enough, if you get what I mean.

MARY. My Peter would never tell a lie, would he? Promise me that.

BUSINESSMAN. Not strictly true? Well, what of it? What's that got to do with it? People don't expect advertising to be true. And here's another thing. I've been going over the books, and I find you've been allowing far too much latitude to debtors. That's got to stop, too. Then there's that little matter of the diffused delivery agreements —

MARY. "Honesty is the best policy." That's the motto I want my big son to have —

BUSINESSMAN. What? Sharp practice? Now look here, Smith, you're not a child tied to your mother's apron strings any longer. It may be sharp practice — I'm not denying it, though if you'd been someone outside the firm I'd have sued you for saying so — but sharp practice is what put me where I am today. And if sharp practice is necessary to keep me there, then sharp practice there's going to be, whether you like it or not.

ANNOUNCER. Here are the latest unemployment figures —

BUSINESSMAN. I may not be as well educated as you are, but I've yet to discover that honesty is the best policy — except for those who are looking for the bankruptcy court.

ANNOUNCER. The total number of persons unemployed at

twelve noon today was three millions, four hundred and twenty-seven thousand —

BUSINESSMAN. Now look here, Smith, you're a good boy. You'll go far if you look at things my way. But I'm just putting you wise — it's got to be my way, or out! Get me?

ANNOUNCER. — six hundred and two, an increase of two on the previous day's figures.

MARY. Then you'll be getting married and leaving your poor old mother. Oh, yes you will! I know! But I don't mind really. . . . Well, I suppose I do in a way, but I'll try not to, for your sake. Especially if she's nice — oh, my precious one, you will be careful to pick the right girl, won't you? Then we'll have a lovely wedding, with the bride all in white satin and orange blossoms and —

(*She goes on talking, but our attention is diverted by the* CLERGYMAN. *He is reading the wedding service to the* BRIDE, *who is kneeling in front of him, all in white satin and orange blossoms, exactly as* MARY *imagined her. We cannot see any bridegroom.*)

CLERGYMAN. Repeat after me. I, Judith —

BRIDE. I, Judith —

CLERGYMAN. Take thee, Peter Ulric —

BRIDE. Take thee, Peter Ulric —

CLERGYMAN. To my wedded husband —

BRIDE. To my wedded husband —

CLERGYMAN. To have and to hold from this day forward —

BRIDE. To have and to hold from this day forward —

CLERGYMAN. For better, for worse —

BRIDE. For better, for worse —

CLERGYMAN. For richer, for poorer —

BRIDE. For richer, for poorer —

CLERGYMAN. In sickness and in health —

BRIDE. In sickness and in health —

CLERGYMAN. To love, cherish and to obey —

BRIDE. To love, cherish and to obey —

CLERGYMAN. Till death us do part —

BRIDE. Till death us do part.

ANNOUNCER. The number of marriages solemnized in churches during the past six months has declined by 40 per cent, states a report —

CLERGYMAN. Judith and Peter, you have just taken the most solemn vows a man and a woman can take. You have sworn in God's house to love and cherish one another till death parts you. I hope you realize sincerely the true significance of that vow, and that you will fulfill it, come what may —

ANNOUNCER. On the other hand, the report records that the total number of divorces granted during the same period was more than 65 per cent above the figure for the previous six months.

(*During the last six or seven speeches,* MARY *has been humming Mendelssohn's Wedding March, as she rocks the cradle gently to and fro. Now she breaks off and speaks to the sleeping baby.*)

MARY. Then you must be very kind to her — but you must try to be firm, too. Remember, a man must always be a hero to his wife —

(*The* BRIDE *has taken off her veil and orange blossoms, and now she bursts into a tirade of abuse.*)

BRIDE. A hero! My God! A fine hero you'd make. Why on earth I was fool enough to tie myself up to you for life I can't imagine. Look at the Robinsons — they've got a car. Look at the Browns — they've got a radio. Look at the Joneses — he takes his wife to Brighton every week end.

ANNOUNCER. The report records that the total number of divorces granted during the same period —

BRIDE. Of course, it isn't your fault. Nothing's ever your fault. As a matter of fact, that's probably true — it's the fault of the way you were brought up. You're too namby-pamby. You won't do anything I ask because you say it's unethical. And what's the result? I have to go about looking like a scarecrow, while Mrs. Robinson has new furs, and Mrs. Brown has a chinchilla coat, and Mrs. Jones has —

ANNOUNCER. More than 65 per cent above the figure for the previous six months.

BRIDE. All right, all right. I admit I was with him. I've been with him lots of times. And can you blame me? He's sensible. He knows which side his bread is buttered. He's got a car, and a yacht, and a bungalow by the river. He can afford to buy me a chinchilla wrap. Of course I was with him! Well, what are you going to do about it?

CLERGYMAN. To love, cherish and to obey, till death us do part —

BRIDE (*in a wheedling voice*). Of course, I want a divorce — but you wouldn't want to divorce *me*, would you? You'll be nice and give me evidence, so that I can divorce you, won't you? All the best people do it that way. You wouldn't refuse me this one thing, would you?

MARY. And you'll never tell a lie, will you, my precious?

BRIDE. Besides, if you divorce me, they won't let me marry Tony in a church — and I do so want a nice church wedding, with lilies and orange blossoms and bridesmaids. You will do it for me, won't you? It's the last thing I'll ever ask of you.

ANNOUNCER. In the High Court of Justice, Probate, Admiralty and Divorce Division, Lord Justice Jackson today made absolute the following decrees nisi: Robinson v. Robinson; Jones v. Jones; Brown v. Brown; Smith v. Smith —

MARY. If anything dreadful should happen to you — like divorce or disgrace — you can always come to me. I'll stand by you. But it won't — oh, Peter, please tell me it won't —

CLERGYMAN. I should never have thought it possible! I always looked on Peter Ulric Smith as such a nice young fellow.

BRIDE. I want you to marry Tony and me — I shouldn't feel properly married if I wasn't married in a church!

BUSINESSMAN. Send in Smith! Smith, you're sacked! We don't want any divorcees here —

SCHOOLMASTER. You must admit a thing like that lets down the school. And I'm told he even wore the old-boy tie in court!

BUSINESSMAN. You say you weren't the guilty party really? It was a white lie, was it? Well, what's that got to do with me? *I* told you to lie? Maybe, but this is the wrong sort of lie, my boy. I've got my reputation to think of — and you can get out and *stay* out!

ANNOUNCER. The total number of unemployed at noon today was four millions —

BUSINESSMAN. That's my last word. You're fired!

ANNOUNCER. — and sixty-seven. . . . I beg your pardon, sixty-eight. . . . The election. Speaking in London today, the prime minister said —

(*Out of the shadows comes the voice of the Politician, and at once a convenient flicker of light picks him out for us.*)

POLITICIAN. My friends, this is a very solemn moment for all of us. The twin specters of poverty and unemployment menace the security of our fair land. Even the richest among us can never be sure when falling dividends and rising taxes may not force us to dismiss our second chauffeur, or third gardener —

MARY. Don't worry about being rich, my precious. Money isn't everything.

POLITICIAN. There is only one way out of this dilemma. We must take what we want, as our fathers took it — and if the world refuses to give freely, then we must take it by force. Our virile young men and women are not going to be denied. They are not going to fall below the high standards of their fore-fathers. Read our glorious history and you will find on every page an epic of heroism, a saga of glory, written in letters of blood and fire. That is the message I bring to you today.

MARY. Money doesn't matter. It's peace that counts. Peace is the only thing in life worth having.

POLITICIAN. This is a democratic country, and I thank God

for it. The decision rests with you. You alone shall provide the answer. Pale peace with poverty in her train — or glorious war with work for men and honor for our nation?

SCHOOLMASTER. History provides the answer — it must be war!

CLERGYMAN. When right is on our side war becomes holy — an act of devotion to God!

BUSINESSMAN. Trade follows the flag — give me war and profits!

MARY. It's peace that counts! Peace is the only thing in life worth having.

ANNOUNCER. War has been declared! (*All of the characters except* MARY *cheer loudly. From this point onward, the speeches follow one another more and more quickly; getting louder every moment; creating an air of tension and excitement.*)

POLITICIAN. War has been declared!

ALL. *WAR HAS BEEN DECLARED!*

ANNOUNCER. The royal trumpeters will now sound the advance. Stand by, please.

POLITICIAN. Men are urgently needed. We must have more men.

SCHOOLMASTER. I'm needed at home to teach the new generation about the glories of war.

CLERGYMAN. My place is to preach that this is a holy war — not to fight it.

BUSINESSMAN. Anyone can fight, but it needs a man like me to see that we make a profit out of the war.

POLITICIAN. Men are urgently needed. We must have more men.

ANNOUNCER. Men are urgently needed.

POLITICIAN. Peter Ulric Smith, your king and country need *you.*

ANNOUNCER. Peter Ulric Smith, your king and country need you.

POLITICIAN. For the glorious destiny of your nation —

SCHOOLMASTER.   For the honor of the old school —

CLERGYMAN.   For the carrying out of God's immutable purposes —

BUSINESSMAN.   For the sake of the profit and loss account —

ALL.   Your king and country need you.

MARY.   No, no! They'd never send you to war! They'd never do that, Peter! Never again!

ANNOUNCER.   Here is the latest bulletin from the front. There was a sharp engagement in zone twenty-four this morning. Casualties were heavy, but neither side could claim any material advantage. . . .

POLITICIAN.   We're doing splendidly. I am confident that victory is in sight.

SCHOOLMASTER.   Our brave boys are performing wonders —

CLERGYMAN.   With God on our side, we cannot fail —

BUSINESSMAN.   Already our turnover has doubled —

ANNOUNCER.   Here is the first casualty list of today's engagement. Killed: Peter Ulric Smith —

POLITICIAN.   Peter Ulric Smith! Dear, dear! A fine boy. Send a telegram of condolence to his mother —

SCHOOLMASTER.   Peter Ulric Smith! Write his name on the war memorial! What a tribute to the training of the old school! Fourteen of our boys have laid down their lives already —

CLERGYMAN.   Peter Ulric Smith! Greater love hath no man than this: that a man lay down his life —

BUSINESSMAN.   Peter Ulric Smith! He used to work for me, but this is the best day's work he ever did. I mean to say, look at my dividends —

ANNOUNCER.   The royal trumpeters will now sound the Last Post. . . .

(*During these speeches* MARY *has risen to her feet and she is now standing, facing the other characters. She is trembling and suddenly she shouts —*)

MARY.   No! You shan't do it! Stop it, I tell you! Stop it!

ALL.   What?

MARY (*shrieking*). Stop!

ALL. Stop?

MARY. Yes, stop! It mustn't be like that! It mustn't! Is that what I've suffered agonies for? Is that the best you can give my son? If that's all the world can offer, then I'd rather kill him now — before he's had time to learn what a mockery it all is. I'd rather kill him, I tell you, than let him grow up — for that! I won't have it, I tell you. Do you hear that? I won't have it. (*All of the other characters begin to laugh derisively.* MARY *listens hopelessly for a moment. Then she shouts, despairingly*) Stop it! Stop it! (*The baby in the cradle begins to cry.*) There! Now you've wakened him. (*She turns and picks up the child. Holding him in her arms, she turns again — to find that the others have all gone. In their place stands the* MADONNA, *a sad-faced, soft-voiced woman, dressed in a blue robe.*)

MADONNA. There! It's all right.

MARY. Who are you?

MADONNA. Just a mother, like yourself.

MARY. Where's your baby?

MADONNA. They killed him.

MARY. Oh! (*She clutches her own baby more closely to her breast.*)

MADONNA. But you mustn't be afraid. I came to reassure you.

MARY. How can I help being afraid? Didn't you hear what they said — that all my baby could look forward to was lying and cheating and despair and unhappiness and bloodshed and death? Wouldn't you be afraid?

MADONNA (*peeping at the baby*). But he isn't afraid. Look, he's smiling.

MARY. That's because he doesn't know. Oh, it was cruel of me to bring a baby into a world like this! I ought never to have done it!

MADONNA. You say that because you haven't learned the true secret of motherhood.

MARY. What is that?

MADONNA. You have to find that out for yourself. It's a strange thing, motherhood. You may be just an ordinary woman — not particularly clever, or wise, or beautiful — but your baby may be a genius, a great musician, or a poet, or a leader of men. You have to teach him everything — how to eat, and how to walk; how to dress and how to talk — and before you know what is happening, he is teaching you. Things you'd never have dreamed of he will teach you. That's the strange thing about babies. They have something in them that doesn't come from you at all, but from outside. And that's the secret of motherhood — that something which makes every baby a potential leader and savior of mankind. One day some mother somewhere will give the world a child which will put everything right. It may be you — or another mother across the street — or across the world. But whoever it is, she won't know — any more than you or I knew. Look at my Son, for instance —

MARY. But they killed him, you said.

MADONNA. That didn't make any difference.

MARY. No difference! I don't want my son killed.

MADONNA. He said, " I will come again." And I believe that he will — in some other mother's child. And perhaps this time the world will be ready for him. Perhaps it is ready now, for yours —

MARY. Is *that* the secret you spoke of?

MADONNA. Perhaps.

MARY. It's too much to hope.

MADONNA. Why? Isn't all motherhood hope?

MARY. But my baby —

MADONNA (*peeping at him again*). He's still awake.

MARY. I'll put him to bed. (*She goes over to the cradle, puts the baby into it and tucks it in. Then she sits down by it again, in the same position as when the play opened, and begins to rock the cradle gently to and fro. The* MADONNA *stands just beyond the cradle, looking out into the distance, and, as* MARY *begins to sing her lullaby again, we can almost imagine that the* MADONNA *is gently rocking an invisible child in her arms, too.*)

MARY (*singing*).

Hush-a-bye, baby, on the tree top,
When the wind blows, the cradle will rock.
When the bough breaks, the cradle will fall;
Down will come baby, cradle and all.

(*She peeps at the baby to see if he is sleeping. Then she sings, more softly*)

Hush-a-bye, baby, on the tree top,
When the wind blows, the cradle will rock.
When the bough breaks. . . .

(MARY *is still singing as the curtain slowly falls.*)

RELIGIOUS DRAMA IN THE UNITED STATES*

Where is religious drama heading? Toward a high art comparable to the great religious tragedies of Aeschylus and Sophocles? Toward a revival of medieval mystery and morality plays? Toward an imitation of Broadway or Hollywood? Toward propaganda plays for various church boards and good causes? Or toward cheap entertainment? It was to find the answer to these questions that the religious drama department of the Chicago Theological Seminary instigated a study. I shall present first a brief summary of the major findings, and then an interpretation of them.

To make the survey geographically representative, we selected six typical areas of the United States: New England, Middle Atlantic, Midwest, South, Mountain, and Pacific. In certain states of each of these areas we further selected about fourteen hundred churches having a membership of two hundred and more. To each of these churches we sent a questionnaire asking:

1. How many religious dramas † were presented last year?
2. Who presented them (adults, young people, children or mixed groups)?
3. When?
4. Why?
5. With what equipment?
6. What plays were presented?

Replies came from 451 churches. Of these, 411, or 91 per

* Revised and reprinted from the *Christian Century*, through permission of the editor.

† We defined a religious drama as "one that has a religious effect upon an audience; that is, it exalts the spirit, sheds light on spiritual struggles, and challenges the will to right wrong."

cent, stated that they had produced a total of 1518 plays during the year, an average of 3.7 plays per church. Only 40 churches reported that they had presented none. (A similar survey in 1930 had disclosed that 75 per cent of the churches were then presenting plays, and the average number had been 3.2 per church.)

What groups presented these plays? Adults presented 37 per cent; young people, 25 per cent; children, 17 per cent; mixed groups, 21 per cent.

When were the plays given? Thirty-nine per cent were given on Sunday evening as part of a service of worship; 16 per cent in the midweek evening service; 16 per cent at missionary meetings; the rest at various other times. Most of them were given in parish houses; a small proportion in the church auditorium.

Classified by seasons: 50 per cent were given at or near Christmas; 37 per cent near Easter; 6 per cent on Armistice Sunday. (A considerable difference is noted here from the results of the survey of 1930. At that time only 32 per cent of all the plays were produced at Christmas and Easter.)

Why did these 411 churches produce dramas? They gave a variety of reasons: 50 per cent checked " for the inspiration of the congregation," 25 per cent " for the education of the players," 20 per cent " to raise money," five per cent " for entertainment."

With what equipment did the churches present these 1518 plays? The majority had only a platform with temporary curtains and makeshift lighting equipment. But 170 churches indicated that they now have a permanent stage with proscenium and curtains. Only 91 answered that they had an adequate lighting outfit.

What was the character of the plays presented in American churches? Twenty-eight per cent were biblical, 47 per cent nonbiblical but religious, and 25 per cent nonreligious. (In 1930, 36 per cent were biblical, 48 per cent nonbiblical, and 16 per cent nonreligious.) Only one church mentioned a medieval mystery play. Not all the churches gave the names of their plays. But the titles mentioned most often — ten times or more — were: "Why the Chimes Rang," "The Dust of the Road," "The Adoration of the Kings and Shepherds," "The Great Choice," "The Nativity," "The Rock," "The Lost Church" and "The First Commandment." However, these well known plays represent but a small fraction of the total number presented. The churches named 410 separate titles, not including 70 "originals," 20 "missionary plays" and 30 classified as "light comedies."

So much for the bare facts. Now for their interpretation. The most obvious conclusion is that religious drama in the United States has reached a phase of large quantity. But when one studies the list of plays produced and visits a few of the productions, an equally significant conclusion emerges: most of our religious drama is still of low quality. Unless that quality can be improved, drama in the churches will be scrapped. That will be an irreparable loss both to the churches and to drama. To the churches, because they will lose the aid of a great art; to the drama, because, as anyone familiar with its history knows, it has reached its highest usefulness when it has subordinated itself in the service of God.

Why so much religious drama?

1. Because many churches have found that it ministers to a definite need. That need is for an emotional interpretation of our daily life. Much of the ministry of the church today is to the intellect only. To young men and women emotionally starved in an industrial civilization, drama provides a medium in which they can feel and dream as well as think. Maxwell Anderson, in his introduction to "Winterset," speaks of the starvation of men's souls in this age of science. "Men have not been altered by the invention of airplanes and the radio. They are still alone and frightened. . . . Science may answer a few questions for them, but in the end science itself is obliged to say that the fact is created by the spirit, not spirit by the fact. . . . We

shall not always be as we are — but what we are to become depends on what we dream and desire. The drama, more than any other art, has the power to weld and determine what the race dreams into what the race will become." When churches see the drama in that light they use it.

2. Because drama portrays life in concrete terms of characters in action. It doesn't argue about goodness; it walks goodness in on two legs. It doesn't present the struggles of our daily lives academically; it re-enacts them before our eyes. Ralph W. Sockman said some time ago: "The man on the street wants a religion which meets him where he is and then has the power to take him where he is not." That is what religious drama at its best does. It interprets and exalts the common emotional experiences of daily life.

3. Because the American people through attendance at theaters have become (forgive the hackneyed phrase) drama-minded. Young adults generally have seen in drama the most powerful medium for expressing themselves and for influencing the public. They have welcomed an opportunity to work in such a medium.

Why the low quality?

Not all the religious drama in the United States *is* of low quality; some of it is high. Perhaps it is making as rapid progress in quality as any other art in conjunction with religion. Certainly a few of the churches studied in this survey have shown discrimination and intelligence in the plays presented during the past year. For example, the Union Church of Bay Ridge, New York, produced last year "The Terrible Meek," "Outward Bound," "Lincoln," "The Importance of Being Earnest," "The Coming of the Prince of Peace," "Why the Chimes Rang." But the fact remains that the vast majority present no such picture. To anyone familiar with modern drama the 410 different titles reported by these churches reveal a poor quality of selection. And anyone who has witnessed as many of these plays as the present writer, knows that their production is usually poor. It has only good intentions to commend it. Why?

1. Because church leaders have little or no vision of what religious drama might be. If any church leader will devote three evenings to reading the plays of Aeschylus or Sophocles, remembering that these immortal tragedies were first produced in the temple as acts of worship, he will have a vision of what great religious drama can be. He will read plays that were developed by the combined encouragement of organized religion and the state — dramas so powerful in their effects on the inner lives of the ancient Greeks that the very name of Athens became synonymous with spiritual sensitivity. That little town of thirty thousand largely through its dramatic festivals developed more great poets than America has yet developed with a population of one hundred and twenty-five million. So important did the people deem these dramatic festivals that during them all business was closed, law courts adjourned, and the jails were opened so that the prisoners could come into the temple and receive there ethical stimulus. The poets who wrote the plays and the actors who presented them were considered ministers of religion during the period of the festival. The plays were so vibrant with life and so universal in theme that they have survived twenty-four centuries. That is what religious drama might be. Few American churches yet have any such vision of it.

2. Because instead of any such vision, churches have seen drama only as a means of visualizing their message of stewardship or the needs of their missionary societies, or as a new wrinkle in religious education or an " expressional activity " that promised to keep young people busy.

3. Because the majority of the churches, with such minor goals in view, have selected only cheap and easy plays. Every teacher of drama, every publisher, is familiar with the plea, " We want something that can be done with only a few rehearsals, something quite simple, and of course without royalty." Is it any wonder that many intelligent people find more to respect

in a good movie than in the average religious drama? A good motion picture producer often works two years on a historical picture, taking meticulous care to see that every detail of setting and costume is faithfully reproduced and the story convincingly told. Yet most churches want to find a religious drama that can be presented with six rehearsals and with little or no expense. Is a religious drama of less importance than one for entertainment only?

Here the objection will be raised: " But we can't afford the better religious dramas. We can't pay the five or ten dollar royalty." This objection must be squarely faced. Take two examples, churches A and B.

Church A says: " Our Sunday evening congregation numbers about one hundred. The offering averages five cents each. That means only five dollars. We are going to present a play to that congregation and we have only the offering to meet our expenses. We must, therefore, keep our expenses within five dollars. Of course we can't pay royalty for a good play." So it chooses a cheap play; cheap usually because it is poor. The congregation numbers the usual one hundred. The offering is just enough to cover the expense of costuming material and make-up. Financially the play breaks even; but the congregation, in spite of its flattering words to the players, is not greatly impressed. Next time it numbers only seventy-five; and then sixty; then fifty. The players become discouraged, give up and drift away.

Church B says: " Here is a good play. It is worth working on. It has a five dollar royalty and we will need ten dollars more for other expenses. That makes fifteen dollars. To raise that amount we must have three hundred people in the church. Do you suppose we can get them? Let's try." And so Church B goes at it. It appoints a business manager. *It organizes not only its cast but its audience.* It puts as much work on the audience out in front as on the play itself. As a result it gets an audience of three hundred which in turn inspires the players. Inspired players in a good play make the audience

want to come again and again. Moreover, Church B arranges
for that play to go out on circuit to other churches in the community. It presents the drama five or six times. When it finally
balances the accounts, it finds that it has met all expenses, and
has a small balance to apply to improved equipment. Better
yet, it has an enthusiastic group of players and an audience
eagerly looking forward to the production of the next play.

The difference between Church A and Church B is the difference between failure and success in religious drama production.

4. Because of unskilled directors and inadequate equipment.
Churches have learned the necessity of having trained choir directors in order to secure good music. Some day they will see
the necessity of having trained drama directors. As for equipment, who knows of a church drama curtain that does not stick
at crucial moments? Or of more than one church in ten which
is able to light its plays as adequately as the simplest theater?
Even the best of acting would be ruined by the average church
stage lighting.

5. Because it has lacked intelligent criticism. The drama of
Broadway has had the benefit of such sophisticated critics as
Percy Hammond, Brooks Atkinson, Burns Mantle and Robert
Benchley. In addition, practically every Broadway play has
a try-out in a small city, and after the try-out the author, producer, director and players hold a clinic in which they rigidly
diagnose every weakness the play has shown, and set about to
correct it. Church drama groups receive no such professional
criticism.

Answering now the questions with which this discussion began :
Religious drama in the United States is not headed toward a
revival of medieval mystery and morality plays, nor toward imi-
tating Broadway and Hollywood. On the other hand, it is not
attaining a quality comparable to that of the great religious
dramas of ancient Greece. We have a theme greater than the
Greeks had. We have a dramatic story unsurpassed in human
history. We have spiritual struggles on the outcome of which

the very life of civilization depends.   We have characters to
portray of a stature that dwarfs the pagan and medieval heroes.
But we treat them all partially and trivially.   We lack majesty.
The bulk of our religious drama still consists of sentimental
plays pious in tone, heavy with propaganda and weak in the por-
trayal of character.   Yet there is a saving remnant made up of
those religious drama groups with high vision, good direction,
adequate equipment and discriminating selection of their plays.
They head toward the development of an art which will some day
become as indispensable as music in the ministry of religion.
In those groups lies the hope of the future.   To them this collection of significant plays is dedicated.

F. E.